DISEASES AND DISORDERS

AUTISM SPECTRUM DISORDER

By Sarah Goldy-Brown

Portions of this book originally appeared in *Autism* by Toney Allman.

Published in 2018 by
Lucent Press, an Imprint of Greenhaven Publishing LLC
353 3rd Avenue
Suite 255
New York, NY 10010

Designer: Andrea Davison-Bartolotta
Editor: Jennifer Lombardo

Cataloging-in-Publication Data

Names: Goldy-Brown, Sarah.
Title: Autism spectrum disorder / Sarah Goldy-Brown.
Description: New York : Lucent Press, 2018. | Series: Diseases and disorders | Includes index.
Identifiers: ISBN 9781534561212 (library bound) | ISBN 9781534561229 (ebook)
Subjects: LCSH: Autism spectrum disorders in children–Juvenile literature. | Autism spectrum disorders–Juvenile literature.
Classification: LCC RJ506.A9 G65 2018 | DDC 616.85'882–dc23

Printed in the United States of America

CPSIA compliance information: Batch #BS17KL: For further information contact Greenhaven Publishing LLC, New York, New York at 1-844-317-7404.

Please visit our website, www.greenhavenpublishing.com. For a free color catalog of all our high-quality books, call toll free 1-844-317-7404 or fax 1-844-317-7405.

CONTENTS

Illness is an unfortunate part of life, and it is one that is often misunderstood. Thanks to advances in science and technology, people have been aware for many years that diseases such as the flu, pneumonia, and chicken pox are caused by viruses and bacteria. These diseases all cause physical symptoms that people can see and understand, and many people have dealt with these diseases themselves. However, sometimes diseases that were previously unknown in most of the world turn into epidemics and spread across the globe. Without an awareness of the method by which these diseases are spread—through the air, through human waste or fluids, through sexual contact, or by some other method—people cannot take the proper precautions to prevent further contamination. Panic often accompanies epidemics as a result of this lack of knowledge.

Knowledge is power in the case of mental disorders, as well. Mental disorders are just as common as physical disorders, but due to a lack of awareness among the general public, they are often stigmatized. Scientists have studied them for years and have found that they are generally caused by hormonal imbalances in the brain, but they have not yet determined with certainty what causes those imbalances or how to fix them. Because even mild mental illness is stigmatized in Western society, many people prefer not to talk about it.

Chronic pain disorders are also not well understood—even by researchers—and do not yet have foolproof treatments. People who have a mental disorder or a disease or disorder that causes them to feel chronic pain can be the target of uninformed opinions. People who do not have these disorders sometimes struggle to understand how difficult it can be to deal with the symptoms. These disorders are often termed "invisible illnesses" because no one can see the symptoms; this leads many people to doubt that they exist or are serious problems. Additionally, people who have an undiagnosed disorder may understand that they are experiencing the world in a different way than their peers, but they have no one to turn to for answers.

Misinformation about all kinds of ailments is often spread through personal anecdotes, social media, and even news sources. This series aims to present accurate information about both physical and mental conditions so young adults will have a better understanding of them. Each volume discusses the symptoms of a particular disease or disorder, ways it is currently being treated, and the research that is being done to understand it further. Advice for people who may be suffering from a disorder is included, as well as information for their loved ones about how best to support them.

With fully cited quotes, a list of recommended books and websites for further research, and informational charts, this series provides young adults with a factual introduction to common illnesses. By learning more about these ailments, they will be better able to prevent the spread of contagious diseases, show compassion to people who are dealing with invisible illnesses, and take charge of their own health.

THE AUTISM PUZZLE

Picture a thousand colorful puzzle pieces of varying shapes and sizes. Each piece looks unique, but it also shares similarities with the other pieces. Like a puzzle, autism spectrum disorder is difficult to piece together. Autism's pieces are the diverse individuals with similar symptoms, which reveal themselves in different ways. As the world starts understanding more about autism, more of the pieces start to fit together. However, like most large puzzles, it is a long and difficult process to put all the pieces together and to see the whole picture.

Autism is a complicated disorder that affects a child's development. For many families, autism brings their child into a new world. The child often stops responding to their name, has trouble communicating, and may show no interest in others. This sometimes makes it difficult for parents to understand their child's needs or thoughts before they learn how their child communicates. For this reason, autism used to scare families because they did not understand what was happening to their child. Some families would send their child away to get help and stop talking to them.

Today, along with an autism diagnosis, families also receive messages of hope. Having autism no longer means that a child will never complete school, go to college, start working, or live independently. Parents now have more resources than ever to help their child reach his or her full potential. Children also start receiving therapy and treatment immediately upon diagnosis. This gives them practice from a young age at working around the challenges their diagnosis presents.

For some, treatment helps them learn to communicate verbally or nonverbally. For others, it helps them learn how to read social cues so it is easier to make friends or have a job. For a small minority of people with autism, the condition may

In 1999, the Autism Society adopted the colorful puzzle piece ribbon as the universal symbol for autism awareness.

even disappear completely as they grow. However, not even doctors can predict the course a child's autism spectrum disorder (ASD) will take. Deborah Fein, a clinical neurologist, explained, "I've been studying autistic kids for 40 years, and I'm pretty good at what I do. But I … can't predict who is going to turn out with optimal outcome … There's so much we still don't understand."[1]

The cause of autism remains unknown, which means autism cannot be prevented. Although there are many treatment options available, doctors cannot immediately pinpoint which treatment will work best for which kids. This causes many parents to spend a small fortune on treatments that may not work. There are also thousands of adults living with autism, but little is known about how the condition progresses with age, and services can be hard to come by.

To help answer some of these unknowns, nonprofits, research institutions, and government organizations such as the Centers for Disease Control

Children with autism play sports, dance, and cheer but may need some extra help as they play or learn a new routine.

and Prevention (CDC) have made autism research a priority. In 2014, President Barack Obama signed the Autism CARES Act. This new legislation funds autism research and will shed light on the challenges faced by individuals living with ASD. Together, all research efforts hope to answer autism's many unknowns.

CHAPTER ONE

A GLIMPSE AT AUTISM

Just before Owen Suskind's third birthday, his parents noticed his development had started to regress, or go backward. Suskind's father said, "He could barely use a sippy cup, though he'd long ago graduated to a big-boy cup. He wove about like someone walking with his eyes shut."[2] Their chatty three-year-old son stopped making eye contact, stopped speaking, and cried uncontrollably. He lost interest in many of his old activities, except for watching Disney movies.

Temple Grandin, who was born with autism and grew up to become a psychologist and advocate for others with autism, described her two-year-old self as "a little wild animal."[3] When her mother tried to hold her, Temple would stiffen up and fight to get away. She felt most calm when left alone and would often sit staring into space for hours. Her mother thought Temple was deaf because she did not learn to speak, nor did she respond when spoken to. She threw temper tantrums and often rocked back and forth or spun around on her toes. She seemed walled off from the outside world.

Donna Williams, at age three, stared into nothingness, too. She could speak, but she could not hold a conversation or share information. Donna also recalled that she heard only "gabble"[4] when people spoke to her. She could not understand what the other person meant and tried to ignore it. She preferred to be left alone and spin in circles or listen to the sound

Children with autism may prefer sitting alone because they find it soothing.

that occurred when she repeatedly tapped her chin with her finger. She said she felt comfortable only in her own world and did her best to tune out the real world.

A Developmental Disorder

Owen, Donna, and Temple are all examples of people with autism. In some ways, they behaved differently from one another, but each manifested severe developmental problems from an early age. This is why autism is defined as a spectrum disorder: Not everyone who has autism behaves the same way. Child development is the complex process of change that all human beings go through as they learn from birth to move, think, feel, and relate to other people. Developmental steps include thousands of changes such as learning to smile at a parent, learning to crawl, learning to walk, learning language, and learning to play games with other children. Within the first three years of life, even though they look the same as other children, the development of children with autism changes. Autism is often called a pervasive developmental disorder because the developmental problems affect, or are spread across, so many areas of learning and relating. The term autism comes from the Greek term *autos*, which means "self." People with autism may seem self-absorbed because they have trouble responding to the world outside themselves.

Autism spectrum disorder occurs in two main areas of development. The National Institute of Mental Health (NIMH) stated, "People with ASD often have these characteristics: ongoing social problems that include difficulty communicating and interacting with others [and] repetitive behaviors as well as limited interests or activities."[5] These characteristics can appear differently in different individuals. For instance, there are different meanings to the phrase "difficulty communicating." One person may never speak at all, while another may be able to carry on normal conversation but will sometimes have trouble expressing their ideas. Children with autism can be different from one another, but all have problems in these areas of learning and growing.

Social Communication Impairment

Social communication is difficult for people with

Trial and Error

For typical people, picking up on social cues is so easy that most of the time, they do not even notice they are doing it. They can generally tell when someone's face and tone of voice are displaying emotions such as happiness, anger, or sadness. They can also often tell when someone is losing interest in a conversation based on body language. People with autism do not understand these signals instinctively, so they sometimes react inappropriately. For instance, they may accidentally insult someone and be unaware that they should apologize because they cannot interpret the person's angry or upset body language.

Because people with autism have so much trouble with social interactions, there is a myth that they do not feel emotions the way typical people do. This is false; they feel the same emotions, they simply have difficulty expressing and interpreting them. They do not try to hurt or annoy people, but it occasionally happens because they are unaware how their words and actions affect others. Many people with autism appreciate being told calmly that what they said or did was inappropriate, as well as exactly why it was inappropriate, so they can avoid doing the same thing in the future. For people with autism, learning how to successfully navigate social interactions does not come as naturally as it does to other people; it often involves memorizing what people's reactions mean.

autism. Some, such as Temple Grandin, seem to resist interacting with other people from birth. As infants, they struggle to get away when they are held. They may either stiffen or go limp when they are picked up. They do not look other people in the eye or smile in response to their mother's face. While they are babies, children with autism may be quiet and passive, or they may cry and scream for hours. Generally, however, their parents cannot soothe them because they do not enjoy physical or emotional contact. Other babies do respond to their parents and caregivers but then withdraw from the contact during the first three years of life, like Owen Suskind. They seem to tune out the world and lose the ability to relate to those around them. Still others may tolerate limited physical contact but have trouble relating to people in other ways.

As children with autism get older, they do not meet

many typical social developmental milestones. They may continue to avoid looking at other people's faces. Many seem more interested in objects than in people. They may have difficulty making friends because they generally find it hard to understand social cues. Many seem to be badly frightened or overwhelmed when they are forced into social situations.

Children with autism may seem to prefer objects to people.

Levels of impairment among children with autism vary greatly. A low-functioning child—one with severe autism—may have little social interaction. For example, they may not imitate other people. If a parent tries to get the child to clap their hands in a game or wave goodbye, the child does not respond. The child neither points to objects nor looks at something when the parent points to it. The child may not notice when a parent or other child is sad and crying or outraged and yelling. Often, the child will ignore people and prefer to be alone.

A high-functioning child—one with less severe autism—may have different social problems. They may be interested in other people but not know how to interact with them. For example, the child may try to play with other children by grabbing toys or even hitting the other children. If he or she can talk, the communication may be overly honest and lacking in sensitivity. The child may criticize playmates' skills or tell the teacher that they are incorrectly organizing the class. Children with autism may be unable to handle being in a group of people and may throw tantrums or run away, even though they want to fit in and be a part of the group.

When children with autism are not able to communicate what they need, they may become frustrated and throw a tantrum.

The inability to socialize appropriately can also be caused by communication deficits in those with autism. People with autism may have serious difficulty with verbal and nonverbal communication. Nonverbal communication is the body language, gestures, and facial expressions that people use to relate to each other. Children with autism have a hard time learning what these gestures and expressions mean, and they may not use them correctly. Some children might avoid eye contact, point to a cookie to communicate that they want one, or nod and shake their head for "yes" and "no." Others may learn some basic nonverbal signals but be confused about others. They cannot "read" the emotions of others and often do not express emotions in a typical way; although they feel emotions, they often do not show those emotions in their facial expressions, which can be confusing to people without autism.

Some children with autism never develop typical verbal communication. According to a study by Boston University, about 30 percent of children with autism speak few or no words at all. Little research has been done on nonverbal autism, so much is still poorly understood about it. Experts are unsure why some people with autism cannot or will not speak; they are studying the brain activity of these people to learn more about it. Nonverbal autism is made more complicated by the fact that it is not well defined. Some people who are considered nonverbal make sounds but never speak true words, some use a few words, and others become verbal as they grow. However, even people with nonverbal autism are often able to communicate in other ways, such as with picture cards, sign language, or typing on a computer.

Other children with autism do learn to speak but might use words in an unconventional way. Some have echolalia. They may repeat exact phrases that are said to them. For instance, if a teacher asks, "Do you want a cookie?," the child responds, "Do you want a cookie?" The child may mean "yes" when they repeat the phrase, but they are often repeating, or echoing, without meaning. They may also use "scripting" to communicate— memorizing certain phrases they can repeat in response to cues they have heard before. For instance, a person with autism may always respond to the question, "How are you?" with the answer, "I'm fine, thanks." They may not actually be fine, but they have memorized this phrase as an appropriate answer to the question.

Children who do develop meaningful speech may still use echolalia to communicate. There are two kinds of echolalia: immediate and delayed. Immediate echolalia is when the person repeats something right after they hear it, while delayed echolalia "is the repetition of phrases after a period of time—several minutes or a year after the phrase was originally heard—and the phrases may pop up any time, any place."[6] David Karasik was a young man with autism who often used delayed echolalia to communicate his needs. For example, if he became upset and wanted to leave a situation, he might say, "Luke! This old man, he played one! Come on, Luke!"[7] He did not know anyone named Luke. Perhaps it was a name from his favorite TV show. He was echoing pieces of language he had heard in the past and using this language to get across his meaning: "Let's get out of here!"

Some people with autism learn to use language in the same way typical people do. However, even they often have verbal communication problems. For example, they may not know how to join in a conversation without interrupting. They may take words too literally and be unable to make sense of a statement such as "That was a piece of cake." To them, a piece of cake may mean dessert, not "that was easy." People who use scripting to communicate may sound artificial when they talk because they are repeating the same exact words every time. However, this does not mean they do not have their own, original thoughts; it simply means they have difficulty communicating those thoughts in their own words.

Philip Reyes, a 14-year-old boy with nonverbal autism from Buffalo, New York, uses a computer to communicate with people. In an article for *The Mighty*, which he wrote when he was 12 years old, he described what having nonverbal autism is like:

> *Let's pretend you are like me. You can't talk, but you have a well-functioning mind and can understand people. Imagine you answer everyone who says something to you, but only you can hear it. Others hear your voice saying things you don't necessarily mean. They think that's all you are capable of thinking ... Meaningful communication means being able to say what I want to say. People must believe we are capable and that our minds are intact.*[8]

Repetitive and Restricted Behaviors

Grandin has worked with experts to help them understand a possible meaning for the second problem area in autism—repetitive and restricted behaviors. Repetitive behavior, or self-stimulation—often called "stimming"—is behavior repeated over and over again, often in an obsessive way. Actions such as spinning, rocking, and hand-flapping are examples of stimming. Experts also call them stereotypic behaviors because

Turning light switches on and off is one example of stimming.

they are performed repeatedly and always in exactly the same way. Opening and closing doors and repetitively turning lights on and off are examples of this behavior. More complex behaviors can be stereotypical, too. For instance, a child with autism may insist on keeping to a rigid daily routine. The child may have a tantrum if expected to eat breakfast before getting dressed if they are used to the opposite and may need to know days in advance of any changes to the routine along with multiple reminders that there will be a change. The child may also have to line up toys in a certain, very neat way before going to bed each night.

Some children exhibit restrictive behavior by needing everything to be neat and precise.

Stimming behaviors seem purposeless, similar to those performed by people with obsessive-compulsive disorder (OCD). However, while people with OCD often perform repetitive tasks to counteract unpleasant thoughts or stop some imaginary harm from occurring, people who stim perform certain actions to help themselves feel better when they are having trouble processing the world around them. For instance, many people with autism are overly sensitive to sensory input, which is the way people experience the world through vision, hearing, touch, smell, and taste. Some have terrible problems with flickering fluorescent lights, brightly colored objects, loud noises, or things that involve using multiple senses at once. Many feel as if they see and hear every detail in the environment and are unable to tune out distracting sights and sounds on their own the way typical people can. Stimming may help them deal with too much sensory input, as well as manage strong emotions or keep them focused when trying to have a conversation. Some typical people find stimming behaviors distracting, especially if they do not understand them, so some therapists believe stimming should be discouraged to make the person with autism seem more "normal." However, many experts agree that as long as stimming behaviors are not physically harmful, there is nothing wrong with them.

Children with autism also typically have specific interests, which they never get bored with. As a child, Owen Suskind enjoyed watching, re-watching, quoting, and drawing characters from Disney movies. Other children might show interest in trains, computer games, or art. Parents and family members of an individual with autism may find it easiest to connect with their loved one by sharing in their special interest. This is how Owen's family and therapists were able to communicate with him, teach him, and learn from him. Even though children with autism can focus well on their special interest, they may struggle to focus on other tasks such as self-care or schoolwork.

Autism and Learning Disabilities

Determining what most people with autism sense, experience, or understand can be difficult, especially when people are unfamiliar with how they communicate. According to the National Alliance on Mental Illness (NAMI), many children with autism

Extraordinary Talent

The skills people with autism have can be impressive. Many people with autism have excellent memories and are able to memorize large amounts of information. Author Daniel Tammet, one man with autism, is shy, rarely looks people in the eye, cannot drive a car, and finds grocery shopping too hard and overwhelming. At the same time, he speaks nine languages, including Manti, a language he created himself. He is a mathematical genius and has been able to solve complex problems in his head since the age of three. Tammet explained that he sees numbers as colors, shapes, and mental images. He said, "When I multiply numbers together, I see two shapes. The image starts to change and evolve, and a third shape emerges. That's the answer. It's mental imagery. It's like maths without having to think."[1]

1. Quoted in Richard Johnson, "A Genius Explains," *Guardian*, February 12, 2005. www.guardian.co.uk/theguardian/2005/feb/12/weekend7.weekend2.

are also diagnosed with some degree of intellectual disability. Experts are unsure, however, if this diagnosis is caused by autistic symptoms or if it is a true intellectual disability. For example, Susan Rubin is a woman with autism who was considered to be severely intellectually disabled until she was 13 years old. At that time, she was introduced to a special keyboard on which she learned to communicate by typing. Susan always understood language; she just never had the tools to communicate. Once she could talk using the keyboard, her doctors realized she was not intellectually disabled. Today, she displays above-average intelligence.

One type of intellectual disability that frequently occurs in people with autism is called fragile X syndrome, which is a genetic condition—passed down in families—that affects a specific gene on a person's X chromosome. According to the U.S. National Library of Medicine, "About one-third of individuals with fragile X syndrome have features of autism spectrum disorders that affect communication and social interaction."[9] This condition is the most commonly identified cause of autism, but not everyone with autism has it, and not everyone who has it has autism. Experts are still studying people with autism to determine other causes.

People with autism who do not speak can still communicate in other ways. Being nonverbal does not mean they are unable to think.

Associated Medical Problems

People with autism may have other serious medical problems too. A seizure disorder called epilepsy is a common condition associated with autism. According to the National Institute of Neurological Disorders and Stroke, roughly 20 to 30 percent of children with autism will develop epilepsy by their 18th birthday. A study conducted by the Kaiser Permanente Autism Research Program showed that people with autism were more likely to have diabetes, digestive problems, sleep disorders, high cholesterol, high blood pressure, and obesity. Other medical problems can include severe allergies, depression, and anxiety attacks. Dr. Lisa Croen, a senior research scientist at Kaiser Permanente, said, "People with autism often have very selective eating and their nutrition suffers … Their social impairments can lead to isolation, which leads to a lack of exercise. So some lifestyle factors can create more unhealthy lifestyles."[10] This is not true of all people with autism, but it is important for researchers to look at anything that might be a contributing factor to certain diseases.

A Unique Disorder

Autism spectrum disorder is not a disorder that is easy to identify. The diagnosis describes a whole range of disabilities that affect many areas of development to different degrees and may also be accompanied by many difficulties. Two people with the same diagnosis may behave completely differently; there is no list of symptoms that every person with autism shares. Today, experts and doctors define autism as a spectrum disorder that must be diagnosed and treated and may have a wide range of outcomes, depending on the individual.

CHAPTER TWO

DIAGNOSING AUTISM

Autism is the well-known term for what is properly referred to as autism spectrum disorder (ASD). In 2013, the criteria for diagnosing autism changed significantly so that doctors could more accurately make a diagnosis. The autism spectrum used to include five different disorders. Currently, ASD is considered one disorder that a person can have in varying levels of severity. All levels of severity describe autistic impairment in the two main areas of social interaction and communication as well as restricted and repetitive behavior.

Diagnosing autism requires clinicians—doctors and other specialists who diagnose and care for patients and clients—to observe a child's behavior and developmental difficulties. Generally, an autism diagnosis begins when a parent notices that their child is not meeting typical developmental milestones. Using different tests, a doctor can diagnose children by the age of three or sometimes even earlier. Early diagnosis is an important goal because the earlier ASD is recognized, the earlier parents can identify which areas their child needs the most help in. Understanding that a child has autism is an important step toward figuring out how best to communicate with them.

Tools for Diagnosis

Typically, a medical doctor, psychiatrist, or psychologist diagnoses ASD. Clinicians must use both their

experience and the accepted standards of diagnosis in the professional community. In the United States, these standards and criteria are established by the American Psychiatric Association (APA) and published in the *Diagnostic and Statistical Manual of Mental Disorders, 5th Edition* (*DSM-5*). Autism spectrum disorder has its own set of criteria that must be met before a diagnosis is made. Clinicians use the *DSM-5* because the medical community agrees that the standards are the best tools available for recognizing and diagnosing disorders.

Recent History of Autism

From 1994 to 2013, the mental health community used the fourth edition, *DSM-IV*, when making diagnoses. The *DSM-IV* allowed clinicians to diagnose children with one of five autism spectrum disorders: autistic disorder, Rett's disorder, childhood disintegrative disorder, Asperger's syndrome, and pervasive developmental disorder–not otherwise specified (PDD-NOS). To receive a diagnosis, a child had to show symptoms in three areas: social interaction, communication, and restricted or repetitive behaviors.

Due to concerns over making an accurate diagnosis, a group from the APA changed the autism diagnostic criteria. Bryan King, a member of this group, said, "There wasn't any evidence after 17 years that [the *DSM-IV* diagnoses] reflected reality."[11] To change this, the group eliminated the five autism spectrum disorders. Rett's disorder has a known genetic cause, so the medical community no longer considers it a form of autism. The new manual, the *DSM-5*, combines the other four disorders into a singular autism spectrum disorder with different levels of severity.

ASD Diagnostic Criteria

Diagnosing ASD requires clinicians to identify "persistent deficits in social communication and social interaction across multiple contexts," as well as "restricted, repetitive patterns of behavior, interests, or activities."[12] To meet the criteria for an ASD diagnosis, the child must show deficits in all three areas of social communication and interaction and at least two out of four areas of restricted or repetitive behaviors. The three areas of social communication are:

- social-emotional reciprocity (sharing interests, holding a two-way conversation, expressing emotion, etc.)

- nonverbal communicating in social situations (eye contact, body language, facial expressions, etc.)

- forming and understanding relationships or adjusting to social settings (making friends, understanding relationships, changing behavior depending on what is appropriate for the situation, etc.)

The four areas of restricted or repetitive behavior are:

- repetitive movements (hand flapping, rocking, echolalia, etc.)

- inflexibility (upset by small changes, rigid thinking patterns, rituals for everyday interactions, etc.)

- restricted interests (fixating on one or two things with unusual intensity)

- unusual response to sensory input (ignoring pain, upset by noise or light, frequently smelling or touching things, etc.)

A child who cannot hold back-and-forth conversations, cannot understand nonverbal gestures, and has no interest in making friends would meet the social communication and interaction criteria. If that same child also becomes upset by small changes and has highly restricted interests, they would also meet the restricted or repetitive behavior criteria. The child's symptoms must take place during early development, affect the child's ability to function, and not be caused by an intellectual disability or global developmental delay (GDD), which is when a child does not hit certain milestones such as walking and talking at the same time as other children their age. GDD is a term that is generally used when doctors are unable to diagnose a specific condition that is causing the delay.

Clinicians also have to note whether the child is "with or without accompanying intellectual impairment," "with or without accompanying language impairment," and "associated with a known medical or genetic condition or environmental factor."[13] Next, the doctor assigns a severity level. ASD has three levels of severity based on the support a patient needs. A child receives a level of severity for both the social communication and interaction criteria and the restricted or repetitive behavior criteria. Level one indicates that a person does not need much support, while level three indicates that they need a lot of support. A child could receive, for example, a diagnosis of autism spectrum disorder with intellectual delay, social communication severity level two, and restricted or repetitive behavior severity level three. This specific diagnosis should help doctors and therapists understand their patients' needs better.

Level One: Requiring Support

Level one is the lowest level of severity of ASD. Individuals who speak in full sentences and communicate their needs but struggle with back-and-forth conversations would receive a level one assignment for social communication. These individuals often have limited interest in engaging with others and a difficult time making friends. A child who has trouble moving between different activities and difficulty with organization and planning would be assigned level one for restricted, repetitive behaviors. Support, whether it is in the classroom, at work, or at home, enables those with this diagnosis to function more easily. With this support, they are generally able to lead the same kind of life as a typical person.

Level Two: Requiring Substantial Support

Individuals diagnosed with ASD who require substantial support will receive a severity level of two. Those with level two severity in social communication rarely initiate, or start, conversation with their peers and do not respond appropriately when others approach them. They may speak using simple words and only interact when the conversation relates to one of their specific interests. Individuals who have inflexible behavior, cannot handle change, and whose

Prevalence of ASD

According to the CDC, more children are being diagnosed with autism spectrum disorder than ever before. In 2014, the CDC reported that 1 in 68 children in the United States has ASD, making it the fastest-growing serious developmental disability in the country. This translates to about 1.09 million people under the age of 18.

Altogether, the CDC estimates that 3.5 million Americans live with autism spectrum disorder. However, autism used to be considered a rare disorder. Some experts say that the way autism is diagnosed has changed, so now more people meet the diagnostic criteria. For example, some people who used to be diagnosed with an intellectual disability are now diagnosed with ASD. An increase in autism awareness is also thought to explain the increase in autism diagnoses. Parents now know what symptoms to look for in their children and can find resources online to help check their child's developmental milestones.

Other experts doubt that changes in the definition of autism have caused the increase. Some say that toxins in the environment, infections, or parents having children later in life is triggering autism. Despite all the theories, the true cause for the increase remains unclear and needs further study.

restrictive or repetitive behaviors affect their ability to function in some areas will also receive a level two diagnosis.

Level Three: Requiring Very Substantial Support

Level three severity includes individuals who need the most support. Their deficits in social communication severely impair their ability to function. They also initiate few social interactions and rarely respond when others interact with them. Many people with nonverbal autism would fall into this category, since it would be difficult for them to make their needs known on a regular basis.

Those who require very substantial support due to their restricted or repetitive behaviors have inflexible behaviors, have a difficult time dealing with change, and their restricted or repetitive behaviors negatively affect their functionality in all areas. Also, they have great difficulty trying to change focus or change what they are doing. They are generally not able to live completely on their own because they often have difficulty remembering how to perform daily tasks.

Social Communication Disorder

Along with a change to ASD diagnosis, the *DSM-5* also created a related diagnosis—social communication disorder (SCD). Individuals who struggle with social communication but not with restricted or repetitive behaviors may receive a diagnosis of SCD instead of ASD. This includes a majority of individuals who previously received a diagnosis of PDD-NOS under the *DSM-IV*. Children with SCD have trouble verbally and nonverbally communicating, but it is not caused by an intellectual disability. People with SCD might not understand jokes made by their classmates. They might also respond inappropriately during conversation, have trouble with social relationships, struggle to advance in school or at work, and have a hard time speaking and writing.

A Parent-Guided Diagnosis

An autism spectrum disorder diagnosis typically begins with a child's parents. More often than not, a parent first notices that the child is not developing as expected and expresses concern to the child's regular doctor. If the pediatrician agrees with the parents, they will refer the child for an evaluation by a clinician with experience in diagnosing ASD. Many pediatricians use a screening tool called the Modified Checklist for Autism in Toddlers–Revised (M-CHAT-R) to look for warning signs of ASD. This checklist is a series of 20 questions for parents to answer and can be used with children between 16 and 30 months of age. The parent answers yes or no to questions about social skills, such as whether the baby enjoys movement activities such as bouncing on an adult's knee. Other questions ask about smiling at the parent's face, making eye contact, pointing at objects, and whether the child seems deaf or oversensitive to noise.

When screening for autism, a doctor will ask if the child enjoys activities such as peek-a-boo.

The pediatrician scores the checklist. If the child fails more than three questions, he or she may be at risk for developing ASD. However, the test is not perfect. One problem with the M-CHAT-R is that it gives many false positives. This means that many children who do not have ASD fail the test. The psychologists who developed the checklist explained that "the threshold for failing ... was set low to avoid as many misses as possible."[14] The goal is to be sure that a child at risk for developing ASD is not overlooked.

Therefore, the developers created an M-CHAT-R Follow-up Interview that provides doctors with more detailed questions that relate to those questions that were failed. For instance, if the parent answered "yes" that the child gets upset by everyday noises, the doctor may run down a list of everyday noises and ask the parents how their child responds. If the interview still suggests real developmental problems, the pediatrician refers the child to a specialist in diagnosing ASD. At that point, a whole team of experts may be involved in the diagnosis. These experts might include a developmental pediatrician, a pediatric neurologist, a child and adolescent psychiatrist, or a psychologist.

Is It Autism?

Once the child is referred, a clinician will interview the parents again. He or she will ask about the child's developmental milestones. In most cases, the clinician also directly observes the child, looking for areas of delayed skills or unusual and autistic behaviors. There is no medical test to diagnose autism. Instead, specialists must make the diagnosis by ruling out related disorders, assessing the child's developmental history, and following the *DSM-5* diagnostic criteria. Many clinicians use a rating scale such as the Childhood Autism Rating Scale 2 (CARS2). Clinicians use the standard version (CARS2-ST) to detect autism in children under the age of six and in individuals who have below-average IQs or problems communicating. The high-functioning version (CARS2-HF) assesses people over the age of 6 who have no communication difficulties and IQ scores above 80. The high-functioning version uses more sophisticated language and assesses more cognitive abilities than the standard version. To gather additional information about the child, clinicians may also use the Questionnaire for Parents or Caregivers (CARS-QPC).

Both the CARS-ST and CARS-HF rate the child in 15 different areas of development and behavior. The diagnostic tool looks at areas such as relationships, verbal communication, activity level, and the clinician's general impression of the child. Each area is scored from 1 to 4, for normal, mild, moderate, and severe. At the end of the assessment, the clinician adds up all the scores and gets a sum of autistic behaviors and their severity. The score ranges from 15 to 60.

Children who score below 30 points are judged non-autistic. Children who score above 30 are autistic, and scores above 36 suggest severe autism.

To score a child accurately, the clinician needs to understand child development and be familiar with autistic symptoms. They must also compare the test scores with the *DSM-5* criteria to decide upon a specific diagnosis. The younger the child, the more difficult this process is, if only because the child has fewer developmental skills to test. Even tests such as CARS2 are therefore still subjective and dependent on the knowledge of the clinician. That is why experts say that no one test can be used to diagnose ASD. The CDC warns, "There are many tools to assess ASD in young children, but no single tool should be used as the basis for diagnosis."[15]

In addition to autism rating scales, clinicians have to get an overall picture of the child's development. A psychologist will test the child's intelligence and cognitive, or thinking, skills. A hearing specialist has to rule out hearing loss if the child acts deaf. A speech and language therapist assesses the child's language development. A medical doctor may need to test for seizures or other associated medical problems. An occupational therapist determines how skilled the child is at activities of daily living. For a young child this might mean toilet training, self-feeding, undressing, walking, playing, or using crayons.

Celebrities with Autism

Autism has always existed, but before 1944, there was no word for it. People with autism were sometimes considered bizarre or even insane before enough research had been done for experts to realize what the true issue was. For instance, researchers now believe the famous composer Wolfgang Amadeus Mozart, who lived in the mid-1700s, had autism, based on historical descriptions of him that say he "had repeated facial expressions and was in need of constant motion of his hands and feet. His hearing was also very sensitive."[1]

Many modern-day celebrities also have autism, particularly the form that was known before 2013 as Asperger's syndrome and is still referred to that way by many people who either do not know or care about the *DSM-5*'s change in diagnostic criteria. Many first realized they had autism when they were adults, often from doing their own research. For instance, director Tim Burton and his wife first believed he had autism when they were watching a documentary about it and he identified with the people in the film. However, Burton has not been formally diagnosed. Dan Harmon, who helped create and write the TV shows *Community* and *Rick and Morty*, recognized the symptoms of autism in himself when he was researching Asperger's syndrome for one of the characters on *Community*. Although it is never confirmed on the show that the character Abed has autism, it is hinted at several times. In one episode, Abed raps the line, "On the spectrum?/none of your business,"[2] which may be Harmon's way of saying that people with autism deserve privacy.

1. Dresden Shumaker, "11 Famous People with Autism," Babble, 2013. www.babble.com/entertainment/famous-people-with-autism-2/.

2. Quoted in John Hugar, "Abed the Undiagnosable: Exploring the Theory that the 'Community' Character has Asperger's Syndrome," *UpRoxx*, March 14, 2015. uproxx.com/tv/abed-community-exploring-aspergers/.

DSM-5 Controversy

When the *DSM*'s autism spectrum disorders section received a major overhaul, many parents of children with autism as well as adults with autism themselves grew concerned. The *DSM* greatly affects how insurance companies, schools, and treatment or therapy providers think about autism. The new criteria are stricter, which will make it more difficult for a child to receive an autism diagnosis. A study completed in January 2011 showed that 25 percent of its participants who qualified for a PDD-NOS diagnosis under the *DSM-IV* would not meet the *DSM-5*'s ASD diagnostic criteria. Many fear that this could mean those who used to be qualified to receive certain services no longer will qualify, especially if institutions such as schools and workplaces will save money by stopping those services.

In school, children with autism might have an aide to help keep them focused and make sure they know what to do.

The new criteria also attach a level of support needed to an autism diagnosis. However, the criteria do not explain exactly what type of support each child needs, what situations they may need it in, or how the levels of support will influence what services the person qualifies for. This leaves many parents wondering how they are going to make sure their child gets all the support he or she deserves. Additionally, many people who have already been diagnosed with one of the separate autism disorders, such as Asperger's syndrome or PDD-NOS, are not happy with the change in their diagnosis. According to *Slate* magazine, at least two petitions protesting the change have been circulated online; one received 8,000 signatures while the other received 5,400. Some parents feel the new criteria "were designed to exclude higher-functioning kids from diagnosis and thereby deny them services,"[16] a claim that has been denied by the APA. Other people are concerned that because many people do not realize ASD is a spectrum disorder, calling all versions of the disorder "autism" may increase the stigma, or negative associations, people have about it.

Other people are unconcerned by the change. Some point out that Asperger's syndrome has always been considered part of the autism spectrum, so not much should change. The group that updated the *DSM-IV* wanted to bring more clarity to an ASD diagnosis. However, many believe that they have just created more confusion and questions. Several groups have begun studies to see whether the new criteria will be helpful or harmful, but the results are not yet conclusive. Two studies that have been completed gave wildly different results: One found that only 10 percent of people who have already been diagnosed would not meet the new criteria, while the other found that 75 percent of people with Asperger's syndrome and 85 percent of people with PDD-NOS would be excluded. More research is necessary to determine whether the new criteria will be helpful or harmful to those with autism.

The Earlier, the Better

Even with the information from a team of specialists, it is difficult to diagnose the severity of ASD or any form of ASD under the age of three. However, diagnosing ASD early is extremely important so parents can figure out how best to help their child meet his or her needs. Some experts are experimenting with diagnostic tools that will allow clinicians to assess risk in babies by nine to twelve months of age. Most autism experts agree that children are probably born with the risk of developing autism, so early diagnosis does seem possible. Clinicians concentrate on improving the diagnosis and treatment of autism, but other experts devote their efforts to understanding its cause.

Doctors routinely screen for ASD beginning at a child's 18-month checkup.

CHAPTER THREE

CAUSES OF AUTISM

Researchers and doctors are still looking for the causes of ASD. Many of these experts have developed theories, but none has been universally accepted as ASD's sole cause, and most people believe there are a number of different possible causes. All experts do agree however, that to understand autism, they have to understand the brain. ASD is a brain disorder, or neurological condition, caused by differences in the way the brain is wired. These changes in the way the brain develops and works could be innate—something one is born with. However, some scientists believe the environment may be involved, too. They suggest that some children are born with sensitivities to something in the environment, such as pesticides, that may adversely affect their brains and trigger the neurological changes that lead to autism.

The Brain's Anatomy

To understand the causes of a brain condition such as ASD, it is important to understand how the brain functions first. Scientists know that different areas of the brain are generally responsible for different activities. The cerebral cortex, also called gray matter, is the part of the brain responsible for higher functioning, such as language, thinking, reasoning, problem solving, voluntary movement, emotional responses, and perceiving the environment. It is the outer layer of the brain. The brain is divided into two halves, or hemispheres. Each hemisphere contains four lobes.

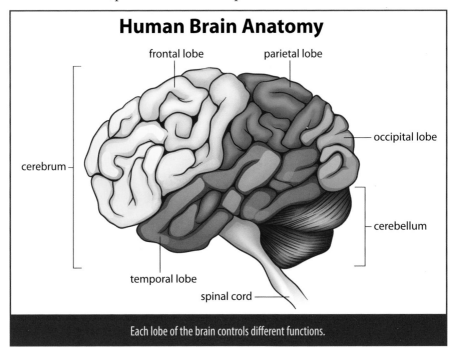

Human Brain Anatomy

frontal lobe

parietal lobe

occipital lobe

cerebrum

cerebellum

temporal lobe

spinal cord

Each lobe of the brain controls different functions.

The frontal lobes are at the front of the brain. They are responsible for such activities as reasoning, speech, problem solving, and some emotional reactions. The occipital lobes are at the back of the brain. They are responsible for vision. The parietal lobes, just behind the frontal lobes, are responsible for perception of pressure, pain, touch, and temperature, as well as for visual thinking and imagination and coordinating input from the senses. The temporal lobes are underneath the frontal lobes. They are associated with hearing and memory. Deep within the temporal lobes is a structure named the amygdala. It acts as the brain's emotional emergency warning system. For example, it is responsible for the "fight-or-flight" response of the body that prepares the individual either to run away from a perceived danger or get ready to fight. The amygdala plays a role in other emotions and in memory, too. All these parts of the brain interact with one another or are wired to and communicate with each other through what is known as white matter.

Focusing on White Matter

The brain is an incredibly complex organ in which different areas communicate and interact with one another. White matter is the nerve fibers in the brain that link all the parts together—that enable the messages to get around. These messages move between the different parts of the brain so that the brain can interpret information and respond accordingly. It is in this white matter that researchers have found variations and abnormalities associated with ASD.

In 2004, scientist Dr. Martha Harber discovered that white matter in autistic brains is larger than white matter in non-autistic brains. However, the increased size of white matter is not consistent—some areas are more expanded than others. She found that there were fewer connections between the right brain and left brain than there were within each half of the brain. This means that information travels better to parts on the same side of the brain, but not so well in parts on the other side of the brain. Dr. Harber believes altered brain wiring could explain why individuals with autism have trouble with social communication, adapting to change, and complex thinking.

Psychologist Marcel Just of Carnegie Mellon University also researches white matter. In 2012, Just and his team measured the white matter in autistic brains and used a computer model to predict how "coordinated" the brain activity would be. Just made the computer function as the autistic brain to complete different tasks. He and his team observed the differences between how the autistic brain and the non-autistic brains solved problems. The model was able to show how the altered brain structure creates

the autistic way of thinking.
Just explained,

> *Social impairments in autism are likely caused by the poor frontal-posterior connectivity. Similarly, language comprehension is performed by a network of frontal and posterior areas, and once again, poor connectivity may impair that network's functioning. This tells us where the problem lies in autism. We can now focus on designing therapies that attempt to either improve the white matter—something we have already proven is possible through behavioral interventions—or help the brain develop work-around strategies.*[17]

Brain Imaging

Scientists can map living brains and observe the activity in working brains by using brain scan techniques such as magnetic resonance imaging (MRI) and functional magnetic resonance imaging (fMRI). These two techniques are described in the following way:

> *An MRI is a medical test that uses a large magnet to create a magnetic field around a person's head. Then radio waves are sent through the magnetic field. A computer reads the wave signals and builds a detailed picture of the brain ... With fMRI, scientists can get an image of the blood flow in the area of the brain where activity is occurring. They can watch the brain as a person does specific tasks, such as solving math problems, looking at faces, or reading. They can see the changes in blood flow that indicate which part of the brain is being used to perform the tasks. They can see how active that part of the brain becomes when it is required to perform those tasks.*[18]

Scientists have used both of these techniques to compare the brains of people with ASD to people without ASD. Their research has suggested several important differences, although no one can be positive about whether the differences are the cause of ASD or the result.

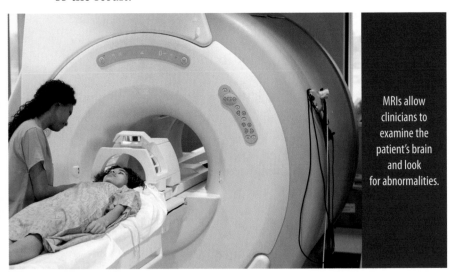

MRIs allow clinicians to examine the patient's brain and look for abnormalities.

Thinking in Pictures

MRI and other tests consistently show that children with ASD show excessive growth of the brain between the ages of two and four. Much of this excess growth is in the frontal lobes. At the same time, the nerve cells that make up the frontal lobes are smaller than normal. No one is sure why this happens or what it means, but psychiatrist Uta Frith, a renowned autism expert, suggested a theory. She explained that, from birth, normal brain development includes a "pruning process" that "eliminates faulty [white matter] connections" and makes the brain connections function more smoothly. Frith said, "Lack of pruning in autism might therefore lead to an increase in brain size and be associated with poor functioning of certain neural circuits [the wiring]."[19]

The wiring that lets the two halves of the brain interact with each other is called the corpus callosum. In 2006, Marcel Just reported discovering that the corpus callosum in some autistic brains was smaller than in typical brains. He also found connection differences between the lobes of the brains of people with and without autism. Just did an experiment in which he asked people to read sentences and score them as true or false. He used fMRI techniques to see what happened in their brains while they worked on the task. The sentences were examples of low-imagery and high-imagery ideas. That is, some sentences were simple statements of facts. Others were statements that make people get a visual picture in their heads when they read the sentences. An example of a low-imagery sentence was, "Addition, subtraction, and multiplication are all math skills." One high-imagery sentence read, "The number eight, when rotated 90 degrees, looks like a pair of eyeglasses."[20]

When people with typical brains read low-imagery sentences, they used their frontal lobes to read and think about the statements. For high-imagery sentences, however, they needed to imagine or see the idea in their minds, and this activated first their frontal lobes and then areas in their parietal lobes. The connections between the lobes were made only when a visual image was needed to decide whether the sentence was true. People with autism responded differently. Whether the sentences were low or high imagery, their parietal lobes were active. Marcel Just and other scientists wrote that this is possibly because people with autism depend on visual brain areas because the connections within the frontal lobes are faulty. Temple Grandin agreed with this assessment. She wrote that she "thinks in pictures." She explained, "Words are like a second language to me. I translate both spoken and written words into full-color movies, complete with sound, which run … in my head. When somebody speaks to me, his words are instantly translated into pictures."[21]

No Quick Fix

Over the years, some people have claimed to know exactly what causes autism and how it can be cured for good. For instance, actress Jenny McCarthy said her son Evan had autism because he was physically sick. McCarthy said she was able to heal Evan's autism. She believed that Evan's digestive system could not process certain foods because it was poisoned by his vaccinations, so she took casein, a protein found in dairy, and gluten, a substance found in wheat, out of his diet. She also gave him large doses of certain vitamins. Evan grew out of his autistic symptoms by the time he was five years old, so some people believed McCarthy's treatment worked. However, many experts believe Evan was misdiagnosed and never had autism at all.

In reality, numerous studies have disproved the theory that vaccines cause autism or that a special diet can cure it. Experts believe several different factors may combine to cause autism, including genetics, exposure to pesticides, and abnormal levels of certain brain chemicals. Scientists know there is currently no cure for autism; symptoms can be treated, but quick fixes—such as a special diet—do not exist.

Increased Sense of Fear

People with ASD seem to use different parts of the brain and use them in different ways than typical people do. The parts of their brain needed to coordinate social skills and emotional relationships do not connect in typical ways. Some studies have shown that the amygdala, which is involved in emotional learning, fear, and sending messages to the frontal lobes, has fewer nerve cells in autistic brains. Scientists at the University of Wisconsin–Madison also found evidence that these unusual amygdalae in children with autism are hyperactive, or over-aroused.

The researchers at the University of Wisconsin–Madison tracked the eye movements of children looking at faces. They made maps of the brain activity that occurred with eye contact. The scientists discovered that the area of the amygdala that signals threats was active when children with autism looked at faces, even when the faces were not threatening. Psychiatrist Richard Davidson, one of the researchers, believes this perceived threat makes children with autism need to look away from faces, which may explain why so many have trouble making eye contact. An atypical amygdala may also explain why so many people with ASD suffer from anxiety—their fight-or-flight response may be activated too much of the time.

Understanding Social Difficulties

Social and emotional responses are controlled by several interconnected areas of the brain, particularly in the frontal and temporal lobes and the amygdala. Scientists theorize that these areas make up the social brain. Because of the social brain, babies are strongly attracted to faces and people, older children use language and play to interact with others, and everyone learns over time to relate to people and understand what others may be thinking and feeling. Many studies suggest that the social brain does not work well for people with ASD because of a difference in wiring. Some studies have found less activity in the frontal lobes of people with ASD when they are asked to describe social situations, such as whether two people are having an argument or enjoying each other's company. In 2007, neuropsychologist Robert Schultz used fMRI to show that the area of the brain that recognizes faces is underactive in young children with autism. However, this same region strongly reacted when children were shown pictures of their favorite interests.

Some studies find that different areas of the brain do not communicate smoothly when people with autism are making social judgments. Marcel Just asked people with and without autism to look at cartoons of different shapes and then explain what they were doing in a social way. For example, one triangle would push on another triangle and nudge it forward. Just was looking for an answer such as "persuading." He used fMRI to measure which areas of the brain were used for the task. He was looking for how well the social areas of the brain were wired together and activated simultaneously. People with autism had trouble with this task, and the different parts of their brains did not work together smoothly, as they did in typical people. This was true even though the people with autism had normal intelligence. Just believes that this faulty communications network "is largely responsible for social challenges in autism."[22]

Genetics and Autism

Understanding the neurological differences that exist with ASD is important, but it does not explain how autistic brains came to be wired in an atypical way in the first place. Most autism experts believe that the answer lies in the genes. Genes are the packages of deoxyribonucleic acid (DNA) that code for how every living thing grows and develops. In human cells, genes are arranged into 23 pairs of chromosomes, with thousands of genes on each chromosome. Genes carry the coded instructions that determine how each individual looks, how their body develops, and how their brain functions. Variations and mistakes in genes often determine whether a person is born with a disease or disorder and what abilities or disabilities that person may possess. Scientists suspect that changes in multiple genes, somewhat similar to typing errors, are responsible for ASD. Finding these genes, however, is extremely difficult.

One way that researchers are discovering the role that genes play in autism is through studying identical twins. Identical twins have almost the same genes. Dr. Thomas Frazier, a clinical psychologist from the Cleveland Clinic, conducted a study in 2014 on twins and autism. His study showed that if one identical twin has autism, the other twin has a 76 percent

Studying twins is one way scientists can work to find a link between autism and genetics.

chance of also having autism. When a fraternal twin has autism, their twin will receive an autism diagnosis 34 percent of the time if they are the same sex. This drops to 18 percent for boy-girl twins. His findings and those of many others strongly suggest that ASD is genetically determined.

There is no single gene for autism; instead, many different genes are involved. In 2008, researcher Christopher Walsh led a team of scientists at Boston Children's Hospital who discovered six genes that were faulty in a group of children with autism. All of these genes function together to code for building and strengthening the brain's wiring. Some of the DNA in each gene was missing or turned off. Other scientists have identified other genes that seem to be faulty in some people with autism. In 2011, research by Dr. Daniel H. Geschwind found that certain genes account for 10 to 20 percent of ASD cases. However, no one has found genetic mistakes that are present in 100 percent of people with ASD. This means, Walsh explained, "we still don't understand the underlying genetics for more than half the kids with autism, so we have a long way to go to understand that, and to understand what non-genetic factors might also contribute."[23]

Three studies supported by the National Institutes of Health (NIH) found that fathers were more likely than mothers to give gene mutations to their child. The studies also found that the father's age determines the number of mutations passed on. The older the father, the more "genetic glitches"[24] he would pass on to his child. These gene mutations significantly increased the child's risk of developing autism.

A father's age can influence whether his child will develop autism.

Biological Sex and Autism

Many more boys than girls are at risk for autism spectrum disorder. The CDC states that the ratio is about 5:1—that is, for every girl diagnosed with ASD, 5 boys are diagnosed. No one is sure why this is so, but British autism researcher Simon Baron-Cohen suggested in 2006 that hormones are the answer. In 2015, Baron-Cohen and his research team measured testosterone in babies while they were fetuses growing in their mothers' wombs. They discovered that "samples from the boys with autism show elevated levels of testosterone, along with other hormones."[25] Baron-Cohen said this is true whether the baby is a boy or a girl, since all girls have some testosterone in their bodies. He said the higher the level of testosterone, the lower the rate of language development, eye contact, and empathy—the ability to understand how other people feel—and the higher the level of attention to detail and interest in strictly defined patterns. He called these traits part of an "extreme male brain."

Other experts disagree with the extreme male brain theory. David Skuse, chair of behavioral and brain sciences at University College London, said the idea that people with autism have low levels of empathy is incorrect; they "can feel others' pain, but they are slower to process this emotion."[26] Other people have criticized the idea, saying that since there is no such thing as a "male" or "female" brain, the theory cannot be true.

Several other theories have been proposed. In 2010, biologist Valerie Hu and her team "found that brains of people with autism have low levels of a protein produced by a gene called retinoic acid-related orphan receptor-alpha (RORA) ... [which] interacts with certain types of estrogen and testosterone found in the brain."[27] Their tests showed that testosterone decreases RORA's activity and estrogen increases it. Since many boys have high levels of testosterone and many girls have high levels of estrogen, this suggests boys may be more at risk for low RORA activity.

In 2017, another theory was proposed by Christine Ecker, professor of neuroscience and brain imaging at Goethe University in Germany. Ecker and her colleagues studied the thickness of the cortex in 98 adults with ASD and compared those measurements to 98 people without ASD. They found that a thinner cortex was related to an increased risk of ASD, and since women generally have thicker cortexes to begin with, they may have some protection against the disorder. However, much more study is necessary to determine whether these assumptions are accurate.

Environmental Factors

Scientists also look for environmental factors. An environmental factor is something that influences living organisms besides a change in DNA. Some examples include climate, diet, chemical or toxin exposure, and stress.

Many of the environmental factors linked to autism have to do with the mother during pregnancy. A study based in California has shown that children born to older mothers have an increased risk of developing ASD. Another study found that pregnant women who had fevers and did not take medicine to treat them were twice as likely to give birth to a child with autism as mothers who did not have fevers or who treated their fevers. A Johns Hopkins research team found in 2016 that mothers suffering from obesity or diabetes were more likely to give birth to children with autism. Research has also found a link between prenatal vitamins and a decreased risk of autism. Mothers who take prenatal vitamins containing folic acid decrease the risk of giving birth to a child with autism by 39 percent.

Women who take prenatal vitamins from the start of their pregnancy lessen the risk of autism in their child.

Some other environmental factors affect babies after they are born. Infants living near areas with a lot of traffic-caused air pollution, such as a highway, are at a higher risk for developing autism. Babies born prematurely—before 37 weeks—also have an increased risk.

All the environmental factors associated with autism only show an increased risk in a child being diagnosed with autism. So far, scientists have not found any environmental factors that directly cause autism.

The Importance of Both

Pinpointing the causes of autism is critically important to all autism experts because treating the disorder depends on understanding the cause. Even if scientists find a genetic cause for autism, it is likely that the genes are affected by environmental factors. To discover autism's causes and to create effective future treatments, scientists need to focus on both genetic and environmental factors.

If autism begins in the womb, then scientists may need to find a way to diagnose children at birth. The earlier the child has a diagnosis, the earlier he or she can start treatment. If genes that interfere with normal brain wiring cause autism, then treatment must concentrate on fixing those genes.

Autism is not curable, but it is treatable. Sometimes, people can even grow out of ASD and no longer demonstrate autistic symptoms. However, no one outgrows autism on his or her own. Early treatment—the earlier the better—is the only way to lessen autistic symptoms and problems and help individuals with autism deal effectively with the symptoms of their condition.

CHAPTER FOUR

TREATMENT OPTIONS

For many medical problems, the treatment plan follows a standard path that works for the majority of patients. For autism, however, many different treatment options exist, and each can lead to severely different outcomes depending on the patient. Catherine Lord, founder of the Center for Autism and the Developing Brain at New York-Presbyterian Hospital, explained, "There is no one treatment that is going to work for all children or one treatment that is going to do everything for any given child over a long period of time."[28] Parents of children with autism have to make choices about their child's treatment plan without any guarantee, even from a doctor, that it will work effectively.

Research into treatment for autism has progressed over the past 10 years, but there is still a long way to go. There are methods that have worked for many children, so parents often start with these. However, many different drugs, supplements, and treatment options promise miraculous cures that appeal to desperate parents. A parent's best option is to do their own research, listen to their child's doctors, and keep trying different methods until they or other professionals start seeing positive results and improvements. One principle that most professionals agree upon is that beginning treatment as early as possible is best for the child.

A strong early intervention program can include at least 25 hours per week of therapy.

Start Treatment Early

According to the Autism Society of America,

> *Early intervention is defined as services delivered to children from birth to age 3, and research shows that it has a dramatic impact on reducing the symptoms of autism spectrum disorder. Studies in early childhood development have shown that the youngest brains are the most flexible. In autism, we see that intensive early intervention yields a tremendous amount of progress in children by the time they enter kindergarten.*[29]

Without treatment, the prognosis, or the predicted future, for children with autism may not be very good. Children with untreated low-functioning autism often grow up unable to be independent and care for themselves. They cannot succeed in regular school. Many remain unable to communicate, unresponsive to other people, and unaware of how to behave in society. In the past, people with autism often ended up in institutions. Because they did not receive treatment as young children, they functioned at a low level. Today, the prognosis for children with ASD is much brighter. These children are treated intensively, with the goal of reducing or eliminating autistic problems that interfere with day-to-day activities. For children with autism today, experts and parents have a great deal of hope and high expectations for change.

ABA Therapy

One of the most commonly used treatment methods is called applied behavior analysis (ABA). ABA is a systematic, step-by-step approach to teaching specific behaviors and skills and reducing negative behaviors that interfere with learning and socializing. Desirable behaviors are rewarded, and undesirable ones are ignored. Records are kept of the child's progress, and, as each skill is learned, more complex skills are taught. The program concentrates on the specific behaviors that are disordered in children with ASD—social communication skills and restricted, repetitive behaviors. Each skill is broken down into tiny steps that can be taught to the child and then shaped and molded into an appropriate behavior. The treatment relies on

During ABA therapy sessions, children often play with toys to learn new skills.

intense, repetitive training. Most children enrolled in ABA programs spend a minimum of 25 hours a week in therapy—both at home and in a clinic or therapist's office. Their daily schedules are devoted to treatment and potentially changing the way their brain works.

ABA is based on the idea that a young child's brain is flexible and changeable. Scientists call this "brain plasticity." It means the brain can reorganize itself in response to learning and new experiences. It can develop new wirings and networks, and it can make up for a malfunctioning area by using other areas in its place. The environment teaches the brain to change and reorganize itself. Brain plasticity is at its peak in the first four or five years of life, when the brain is growing rapidly. That is why experts emphasize treatment for children with autism as early as possible. The first few years are the critical time when ABA therapy can do the most good. ABA therapists take advantage of early brain plasticity, said autism expert Geraldine Dawson, to "guide brain and behavioral development back to a normal pathway."[30]

ABA Controversy

Despite its successes, ABA therapy is also controversial. Neurodiversity advocates believe that neurological differences stem from a normal, natural change in genes. They believe that autism, OCD, attention deficit hyperactivity disorder (ADHD), and other neurological conditions are normal variations in human brains. They support people who seek treatment for their disorders but reject the idea that there is something naturally wrong with them that needs to be "fixed" or "cured." Neurodiversity advocates want to treat autism in ways that focus on building up the person with autism. They do not like treatments that focus on stopping arm flapping or encouraging eye contact.

Julia Bascom, executive director of the Autistic Self Advocacy Network (ASAN), explained,

We're [neurodiversity advocates] big supporters of speech therapy or occupational therapy, where the focus is on supporting someone to gain skills or find accommodations. ABA therapy is another story; the stated end goal of ABA is for the autistic child to become "indistinguishable from their peers," and we just don't think that's an ethical goal.[31]

Additionally, as with all autism treatments, ABA may not work for some people. Philip Reyes wrote about the time he spent in an ABA school: "I had to do my drills over and over until I was bored and frustrated with my teachers. Then I would have meltdowns. For me, ABA is not a solution."[32] Some people with autism may try several solutions until they find the one that works best for them.

Early Start Denver Model

Another method commonly used for early intervention is the Early Start Denver Model (ESDM). Typically used with children one to four years old, this model combines ABA with a relationship-focused developmental model. Children with autism generally withdraw from social interaction. They often do not respond when others try to talk to them and do not start conversations. Eventually, parents, teachers, siblings, and other children often stop trying to engage with the child because they either seem upset or do not respond. ESDM's goal is to increase the amount of social interactions a child with autism has so the child has more opportunities to learn. To do this, the therapy focuses on the relationship between the person giving the therapy and the child. It also focuses on how the adult responds to the child.

Elephant Therapy

Although scientists have no evidence that it helps, some parents choose animal therapy, such as playing with dogs, dolphins, or horses, to treat their child with autism. Some parents in Thailand are choosing elephant therapy. During this therapy, children complete different activities aimed at developing specific skills. Feeding and brushing the elephant can help the children overcome their dislike of certain textures or stickiness. Kicking around a ball with an elephant brings the children together and encourages group activity. Riding the elephant helps the child to focus on body control and balance.

Nuantanee Satiansukpong, head of occupational therapy at Chaing Mai University, explained that the elephants' size and ability to do many things holds the attention of children with autism. This makes them engaged in the activities and open to communicating. Some are skeptical about animal therapy, but many parents say it works. The project's founder, Wittaya Khemnguad, said families "see improvements after the elephant therapy and that gives them this hope."[1]

Some parents believe working with animals such as elephants or dolphins can help their children with autism. Hippotherapy is a type of physical therapy involving horses that may help improve autistic children's communication and motor skills.

1. Quoted in David Freeman, "Elephants Help Autistic Children in Thailand," CBS News, May 13, 2011. www.cbsnews.com/news/elephants-help-autistic-children-in-thailand-pictures/.

ESDM addresses topics such as self-care, joint attention, language, motor skills, interaction, imitation, and play. Unlike other models, it is also suited for any environment—including home, school, office, and therapy room. The therapist and the child both feed off each other to determine the direction of a therapy session. For example, if the therapist tries to get the child to play a game but the child wants to lie on the floor, the therapist adjusts his or her plan. Instead of trying to get the child to play the original game, the therapist might create a new game. The therapist might lie down on the floor like the child, then stand up and jump up and down. The goal is to get the child to mimic the therapist's actions. This becomes a new game for them to play.

To help therapists, the ESDM model provides a method for changing the approach if the child does not respond well. ESDM methods are also updated to match the current scientific understanding of language development and child development. For best results, children should receive at least 20 hours of therapy each week—15 hours with a trained therapist and 5 hours with one or both parents.

Scientifically Proven

ESDM is the best-studied early intervention model that focuses on development. In 2012, *TIME* magazine named ESDM one of the top 10 medical breakthroughs of the year. This honor came about because a study showed ESDM normalizes the parts of the brain associated with autism symptoms. Researchers assigned 24 children to undergo ESDM therapy for 2 years and 24 children to undergo conventional therapies such as ABA. At the end of that time, the scientists measured the electrical activity in the children's brains as they looked at faces and at toys. The conventional therapy group responded more to toys than to faces. The ESDM group responded more to faces than to toys—the same reaction typical children have. The researchers concluded that ESDM improved the children's social behaviors, which caused the typical brain patterns. These children also made larger gains in intelligence, lessening autistic symptoms, living skills, and language than the other group.

Meet Them Where They Are

Since ABA and ESDM do not help all children with autism, some parents choose additional treatment methods. One of these methods is DIRFloortime. DIR stands for Developmental, Individual-Differences, and Relationship-Based model. The name indicates that this treatment method does not emphasize teaching specific skills or behaviors. Instead, it stresses meeting each child on his or her level, understanding the child's feelings, and making emotional connections so that the child wants to learn. It tries to help the child reach developmental milestones by connecting with the child and interacting in a nonthreatening way. "Floortime" reflects the idea that parents get down to the child's level, often sit on the floor with the child, and interact only in ways that are comfortable for the child.

During DIRFloortime therapy, parents sit on the floor with the child and play with them.

Psychiatrist and autism expert Stanley Greenspan, who established the Interdisciplinary Council on Developmental and Learning Disorders (ICDL), developed DIRFloortime. The method recognizes six developmental stages that children go through during the first few years of life. Typical children automatically meet these milestones, but children with autism need help. The ICDL website explains that the treatment is aimed at teaching parents to "follow the child's natural emotional interests" and understand "the importance of their emotional relationships with the child."[33]

Achieving Developmental Milestones

The first milestone for a baby is learning to cope with all the sensory information in the world. No matter how old a child with autism is, parents and Floortime therapists start here if the child is stuck at this level. The child may be oversensitive or unresponsive to stimulation. If the child is oversensitive, the parents may be advised to touch him or her gently, to speak quietly and slowly, and to try to help the child be calm. If the child is unresponsive, the parents may encourage interest in the world by talking loudly, swinging or tossing the child, and acting excited.

The second milestone involves making eye contact and responding to a parent's voice. A child who has not accomplished this step may need to play gentle peek-a-boo games for hours to become comfortable with looking at faces. With older children, the parent may get down on the floor and join the child in an activity—even if it is just pushing a toy car back and forth.

The third stage is learning two-way communication. First, this communication is through gestures and sounds. Parents and therapists teach this skill by reacting and responding to anything the child does. For example, if the child waves his or her arms, the parents "ooh" and "ahh" and wave their arms in response. The child learns that he or she has the "power to make things happen."[34] In the fourth stage, the communication grows more complex. The child is encouraged to learn more gestures and to understand the parents' gestures and noises. The fifth developmental milestone involves play. Pretend play helps a child to understand emotions and to form ideas about the world. To feel accepted, a child at this level needs patience and positive support for the stereotyped ways he or she plays with toys. In addition to praising and being interested in the child's play, the parents follow the child's lead and encourage curiosity.

The sixth and final milestone of development involves connecting play with the real world and developing logical thinking. Parents sit on the floor and play with their child. Each time a child makes a silly comment, the parents respond as a way to join in on the child's game. The goal is to have the child respond to the parents' comment to start the process over again. This helps connect the child to their parents and helps connect the child's play to reality.

According to ICDL, DIRFloortime helps many children with ASD make dramatic progress and relate to other people. This treatment is popular with parents, and many professionals believe it is worth trying. The proof that it works, however, is only in parents' or therapists' stories. The therapists have kept careful records that document the children's behavioral progress, but, so far, no independent scientific studies back up these reports.

Unproven Treatment Methods

Alternative treatments for ASD have even less support in the scientific community than DIRFloortime does. Nevertheless, many parents embrace these so-called alternative treatments. They and some professionals believe that autism can be healed with diet, nutrition, and medicines.

Many parents use a special medical treatment, chelation therapy, to "detoxify" their children's bodies. This treatment involves injecting the child with

Know the Warning Signs

The Association for Science in Autism Treatment (ASAT) reports that many treatments for ASD are not based on any evidence and are worthless. The warning signs of false, or pseudoscientific, treatments are:

1. High "success" rates are claimed.
2. Rapid effects are promised.
3. The therapy is said to be effective for many symptoms or disorders.
4. The "theory" behind the therapy contradicts objective [scientific] knowledge (and sometimes, common sense).
5. The therapy is said to be easy to administer, requiring little training or expertise.
6. Other, proven treatments are said to be unnecessary, inferior, or harmful.
7. Promoters of the therapy are working outside their area of expertise.
8. Promoters benefit financially ... [from] the therapy.
9. Testimonials, anecdotes, or personal accounts are offered in support of claims about the therapy's effectiveness, but little or no objective evidence is provided.
10. Catchy, emotionally appealing slogans are used in marketing the therapy.
11. Belief and faith are said to be necessary for the therapy to "work."
12. Skepticism and critical evaluation are said to make the therapy's effects evaporate.
13. Promoters resist objective evaluation ... by others.
14. Negative findings from scientific studies are ignored or dismissed.
15. Critics and scientific investigators are often met with hostility, and are accused of persecuting the promoters [or] being "close-minded."[1]

1. "Pseudoscientific Therapies: Some Warning Signs," Association for Science in Autism Treatment. www.asatonline.org/research-treatment/making-sense-of-autism-treatments-weighing-the-evidence/pseudoscientific-therapies-some-warning-signs/.

chemicals that bind with metals such as mercury and remove them from the body. Other parents try hyperbaric oxygen therapy. It uses oxygen at high pressure in a chamber where the child lies. The idea is that pure oxygen can heal wounds and reduce inflammation in the body. According to the Food and Drug Administration (FDA), both chelation therapy and hyperbaric oxygen therapy carry significant health risks and have no effect on a person's autism.

CHAPTER FIVE

LIFE WITH AUTISM

Parents and guardians of children with ASD can recall instances when they first noticed signs of autism in their child. They can tell stories and compare their autistic child's development to their typical child's development. However, these parents cannot explain what their child feels like as an autistic individual. To learn that, the world must rely on adults and children with autism who are able to explain what life is like living with ASD.

Temple Grandin has spoken at autism awareness conferences to share her life story.

The Importance of Understanding

Donna Williams is one adult with autism who has the ability to explain the pain, fear, and confusion that her disorder caused her. As she grew, she was able to make progress and learn, but it was a terrible ordeal because her development was not typical. She remembered her struggle to respond to the "real world" during her school years, when the only place she felt comfortable was in the world inside her own mind. She was aware that she was different from other children and was afraid of being punished for it. Growing up, Donna's family treated her poorly and she did not have access to therapy. She was not even diagnosed with autism until she was an adult. For Donna, autism was accompanied by fear of a foreign and unforgiving world. This shows the importance of identifying and treating autism early, as well as continuing scientific research into the disorder and spreading awareness about it, especially to typical people.

Communication Is Key

Although many people with autism are nonverbal, that does not mean they cannot communicate. They communicate in their own way, generally through behavior. Tantrums, hitting, and other bad behaviors are often ways children with autism get people's attention when they do not know how to make their needs known. Dr. Lynn Kern Koegel, an autism expert, gave an example:

> Kelly, an adorable little three-year-old, used to bite his fingers so hard there was scar tissue at the bottom of each finger. Telling him to stop didn't help—he'd just go back to biting. So we started keeping track of when he was biting, and we realized it was when he wanted something—it was simply his way of getting it. So, whenever he started to bite, we prompted him to use his words ... Pretty soon, language had replaced biting when Kelly wanted something—it had simply become more effective for him to ask than for him to bite.[1]

Each person with autism may have a different way of communicating. For instance, Koegel also discussed a boy who would knock his mother's glasses off her face whenever he wanted her attention. Once parents and therapists understand the particular way a person with autism communicates, they can work on replacing bad behaviors with good ones. For people with autism who never learn to speak, those behaviors will still be nonverbal, but they will not harm the person or others.

1. Lynn Kern Koegel, Ph.D., and Claire LaZebnik. *Overcoming Autism.* New York, NY: Penguin, 2005, p. 77.

Finding Comfort

Temple Grandin had a different family life from the one Williams endured. Her mother fought fiercely to understand and help her daughter. A favorite aunt was willing to do anything necessary to make Temple's life easier. The little girl developed, learned how to talk, and was able to go to school. However, Grandin also described coping with a lot of fear and stress. She was not frightened of her family or teachers, but her autism left her in near-panic much of the time. When she reached adolescence, she began to have unbearable attacks of fear and anxiety. She believes that this distress is related to her sensory problems. She explained, "As far back as I can remember, I always hated to be hugged. I wanted to experience the good feeling of being hugged, but it was just too overwhelming … Being touched triggered flight; it flipped my circuit breaker. I was overloaded and would have to escape, often by jerking away suddenly."[35]

While Grandin was still a young teenager, she visited her Aunt Ann on her ranch in Arizona. During the visit, she noticed the cattle being put, one at a time, into a squeeze chute, which held them still so that they could be given vaccinations. Immediately, the young girl was fascinated by what she saw. She had always loved animals, and she paid close attention to the cattle's reactions. Many of them seemed to get calm when the bars of the chute were squeezed together around their bodies. She wrote, "The squeeze chute probably gives cattle a feeling like the soothing sensation newborns have when they're swaddled, or scuba divers have underwater. They like it."[36]

At the time, Temple did not think about why the cattle relaxed, but she connected their calmness to her own needs. A few days after she watched the cattle in the chute, she had a terrible panic attack. It felt awful. At that time, she wrote, "My life was based on avoiding situations that might trigger an attack."[37] She decided to try the chute that had helped the cattle calm down. She wrote,

> *I asked Aunt Ann to press the squeeze sides against me and to close the head restraint bars around my neck. I hoped it would calm my anxiety. At first there were a few moments of sheer panic as I stiffened up and tried to pull away from the pressure, but I couldn't get away because my head was locked in. Five seconds later I felt a wave of relaxation, and about thirty minutes later I asked Aunt Ann to release me. For about an hour afterward I felt very calm and serene. My constant anxiety had diminished. This was the first time I ever really felt comfortable in my own skin.*[38]

When her summer vacation ended, Temple returned to school and persuaded a teacher to help her build her own squeeze machine. Today, decades later and despite the fact that she functions like a typical person in the world, she still uses her squeeze machine to help feel calm and in control. Other people may think Grandin's squeeze machine is bizarre, but for her, it is one important way that she adjusts to the demands of the world of typical brains. She knows that her brain works differently, but she wrote, "If I could snap my fingers and be non-autistic, I would not. Autism is part of what I am … I have found my place along the great continuum."[39]

The Role of Technology

Grandin is one of the most famous people with autism alive today. She is a professor of animal science at Colorado State University and often gives public talks about autism. A movie about her life, which starred Claire Danes, was released in 2010. It shows how her logical, autistic brain helped her create brilliant innovations in the field of animal science.

One reason why Grandin is famous is because she was one of the first people to explain to people with typical brains how some people with autism see the world. However, thanks to the availability of personal computers in the 21st century, many people with autism have been given the opportunity to share their own thoughts. Some people with nonverbal autism use computers to share their thoughts; others may be able to speak but still use computers to create blogs about their experiences. Additionally, computers have helped advance autism treatment. Programs have been created to help people with autism recognize emotional cues, and electronic communication such as texting and e-mail help people with autism communicate more effectively because they have more time to think about what they want to say before they respond.

Video games have also been found to have significant benefits for people with autism. Studies have shown that people with autism can focus better and learn more when they are looking at something rather than hearing it. Some games and apps have been developed to help improve social skills and reduce repetitive behaviors. Some people are concerned that people with autism may come to rely too much on technology and use it in place of social interactions. However, the benefits of computers far outweigh these risks, which can be minimized if parents and guardians set limits on computer time.

Finding Independence

The majority of adults with autism today grew up without early intervention or appropriate treatment. Many have no language; live with their parents or in special homes; and are unable to understand social interactions, so they cannot protect or stand up for themselves.

The minority of adults living with autism today

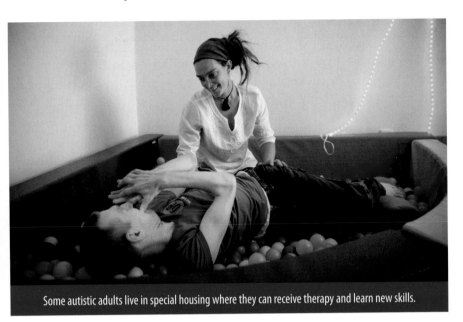

Some autistic adults live in special housing where they can receive therapy and learn new skills.

did grow up with early intervention and other services. Some of these adults have found ways to achieve independence, but not all. Twenty-four percent of adults with autism, mostly higher-functioning individuals, are independent drivers. Those who cannot drive may find independence by learning how to use public transportation. Only 17 percent of adults with autism who are 21 to 25 years old live independently. For comparison, 66 percent of young adults with learning disabilities such as dyslexia live on their own. A 2012 study that was published in the journal *Pediatrics* showed that only 35 percent of adults with autism had attended college or held a job in the 6 years after high school. College is a possibility for adults with autism, but it can be challenging to find colleges that are willing to work with these students. Many adults with autism desire independence, but right now, there are not enough resources or opportunities to make this possible for everyone.

What about the children with ASD who are growing up now? The hope of parents, professionals, and

Almost a quarter of adults with high-functioning autism have their driver's license.

people with autism themselves is that their futures will be different. They hope that new policies and research can provide more opportunities for adults with autism. More importantly, they hope that their differences will be tolerated and even valued by society and that their autism will not prevent them from leading full, independent lives.

Making Learning Fun

Some programs have been created to help young people with autism learn social skills while having fun and making friends. For instance, the Autism Project sponsors a two-week summer camp where participants can experience the fun of camping while also learning relaxation techniques, communication skills, and language comprehension. Programs such as this exist all over the country. Community Connections, another summer camp program, defined the areas that are targeted:

- *Following directions*
- *Attending to and participating in group-based activities*
- *Offering task-relevant contributions*
- *Requesting and accepting assistance*
- *Keeping organized*
- *Completing homework[1]*

1. "Community Connections," The Summit Center, 2017. www.thesummitcenter.org/what-we-do/behavioral-health-division/summer-programs/community.

Laws for Schools

Several laws have been passed to protect students with disabilities and help them achieve good grades in school. One law, called the Individuals with Disabilities Education Act (IDEA), requires public schools to create an Individualized Education Program (IEP) for every child who takes special education classes. The IEP is a legal document that "is meant to address each child's unique learning issues and include specific educational goals ... The school must provide everything it promises in the IEP."[40] The document tracks a student's progress, their educational goals, and what the school will do to help them meet those goals. When a student turns 16 years old, they have the option to attend IEP meetings with their parents and the teachers and officials who oversee their IEP. At these meetings, the IEP team develops a transition plan that will help prepare the student for life after high school.

Another law, called Section 504 of the Rehabilitation Act, also gives protection to students with disabilities, but it is more general than the IEP. A 504 plan outlines what accommodations the student will receive from the school. However, a 504 plan does not have things it must include, unlike an IEP, which has specific areas that must, by law, be included. Additionally, the definition of "disability" is broader under Section 504 than IDEA, so a child who does not qualify for an IEP may still qualify for a 504 plan. Qualification is determined through evaluation by school officials. The disability must be severe enough to prevent the child from learning effectively in a normal classroom environment to qualify for either an IEP or a 504 plan.

A third law, called the Americans with Disabilities Act (ADA), protects people with disabilities from discrimination in the workplace as well as at private schools, including universities, that receive money from the federal government. All three of these laws help people with autism get the most out of their school experience and ensure that they have access to the accommodations they need.

CHAPTER SIX

THE ROAD TO A CURE

ASD leaves many parents feeling desperate for a cure. Autism organizations around the world spend millions of dollars each year funding research—many of these dollars going to researchers looking for that cure. Many believe finding a cure involves first discovering the concrete causes of autism. Others focus their efforts on specific treatment plans. Still others prioritize diagnosing ASD in babies to increase the chance of reversing its effects.

Despite all of these efforts, the path to finding a cure for autism has many challenges ahead. Unlike campaigns to find cures for diabetes or cancer, not everyone wants to find a cure for autism. For many, autism is not just a diagnosis—it is part of their identity. For these individuals, a world without autism means a world without them. Neurodiversity advocates such as Temple Grandin want the world to accept those with autism just as they are, instead of wishing they were someone else.

Focused on Research

Autism Speaks is the largest autism support group and fundraising organization in the United States. Its mission is to change the future for people with ASD. Its website says it is "dedicated to promoting solutions, across the spectrum and throughout the lifespan, for the needs of individuals with autism and their families through advocacy and support;

increasing understanding and acceptance of autism spectrum disorder; and advancing research into causes and better interventions for autism spectrum disorder and related conditions."[41] In 2014, Autism Speaks donated $21.2 million in research grants to studies focused on the diagnosis, prevention, and treatment of ASD and on supporting individuals with ASD. That same year, Autism Speaks collaborated with Google to launch MSSNG, which is a project that "calls for sequencing the DNA of 10,000 families where one or more members is affected by autism."[42] So far, this has led scientists to find new genes that are related to autism. Eventually, this information could help doctors create specialized treatment plans and possibly cures for their patients with autism.

The M.I.N.D. Institute

The researchers at the University of California, Davis M.I.N.D. Institute share the goals of Autism Speaks and are partially funded by the organization. In 2006, the M.I.N.D. Institute launched the Autism Phenome Project (APP) in hopes of better defining and understanding autism spectrum disorder. APP is a long-term study comparing children of the same age with and without ASD. The study examines the children's phenotypic traits. A phenotypic trait is an observable characteristic such as size, eye color, hair color, or skin color. The APP looks specifically at the way the child's brain functions, the brain's structure, the child's immune system, and the child's behavior. The scientists also track the child's diet, other medical problems, and progress in learning.

So far, the APP has collected the largest amount of data on children with ASD ever. Scientists have already learned some new information about autism but also have a lot more data to analyze. The APP has shown concrete differences between the altered brain development of boys and girls with autism. This suggests that treatment methods for girls might differ from methods that work with boys. They have also seen cases where the immune system in the child with autism is different from the parents' immune system. Scientists are doing further studies to see if this could be a cause of autism.

Even within the autism spectrum, these researchers believe that more subtypes of autism can be identified. The director of the study, David G. Amaral, said, "We have come to believe that autism is not a single disorder but rather a group of disorders ... Each one of these autisms may have a different cause. We also think that each type of autism will most benefit from different types of treatment."[43] In the future, accurate diagnosis of the subtypes of autism may point clearly to the best treatment method for each individual child with autism. The scientists at UC Davis hope to do more than develop new diagnostic categories. They want to pinpoint the causes of the autism subtypes, which will lead them to new treatment methods specific to each autistic subtype.

The M.I.N.D. Institute is also launching a new study called the Girls with Autism Imaging of Neurodevelopment (GAIN) Study. This study will focus on girls between the ages of two and three and a half who have ASD or are typically developing. Scientists hope to learn more about the biology of autism in females. Along with this study, the M.I.N.D. Institute is relaunching its APP study. This new study will only focus on boys aged two to three and a half. The children will undergo an MRI scan as they sleep and have some bloodwork done. To find even more answers, the children who participated in the first APP study will take part in a new study called APP-Middle Childhood. M.I.N.D. researchers hope to learn more about how autism develops over time.

In 2003, M.I.N.D.'s Irva Hertz-Picciotto and Robin Hansen launched the Childhood Autism Risks from Genetics and the Environment (CHARGE) study. These scientists hope to uncover the different environmental causes and risk factors for autism. To do this, they look for changes in the genes of children with autism; they also look for such factors as any toxins in their environments, whether their mothers were exposed to toxins during pregnancy, what sicknesses the child has, and which foods the child first ate. They look for medical or biological problems that may affect brain development. They measure fats in the blood such as cholesterol, check how the children's immune systems work, and examine the brain chemicals that affect the brain's wiring. So far, the CHARGE study has identified links between the environment, genes, and autism. The study showed that a mother who has certain genes and does not take prenatal vitamins has a higher risk of having a child with autism.

Starting in the Womb

In 2010, the researchers at the M.I.N.D. Institute reported that they had found a significant abnormality in the immune systems of some mothers who gave birth to children with autism. The immune system is the body's complex method of protecting itself from diseases and foreign invaders, such as germs. When the immune system has successfully fought off an invader, it produces antibodies that can be found in the blood. Sometimes the immune system goes awry and attacks something that is not foreign. This can cause diseases in which the body seems to attack itself. In the case of the mothers of children with autism, the immune system seemed to have attacked the baby as it was growing within the mother. The antibodies seemed to be reactions to a protein in the growing baby's brain. Around this same time, researchers at Tufts University discovered the same antibodies in mothers they were studying. What these antibodies do and why they formed is still a mystery. However, the scientists did discover the children had a particular kind of autism. They seemed to develop normally after birth and then regress. These children may represent the cause of one subtype of autism.

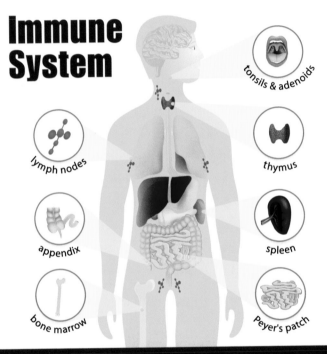

Immune System

tonsils & adenoids

lymph nodes

thymus

appendix

spleen

bone marrow

Peyer's patch

Problems with a pregnant woman's immune system may cause one type of autism.

Identifying the antibodies is important because they can be found in a simple blood test. That means that some children at risk for autism could someday be diagnosed at birth. Many scientists believe that treating children in the first year of life could stop autism in its tracks. Of course, the blood test would work only for those children within this particular autism subtype, but the scientists are excited to have already found evidence of one autism marker.

Dispelling the Vaccine Rumor

In 2009, the courts ruled against parents who claimed a vaccine-autism link existed. These parents argued that mercury in older vaccines and the measles-mumps-rubella (MMR) vaccines caused autism in their children. Despite the ruling, many parents continued to believe that a link between autism and vaccines existed. They believed that children receive too many vaccinations before their second birthday or too many in one doctor's visit and that this could cause autism. Many people who believe this cite a 1998 study by Dr. Andrew Wakefield in which Wakefield claimed he had found evidence linking vaccines and autism. However, this link has been investigated many times since then, and no evidence has been found to back up this claim. In 2004, it was revealed that Wakefield's study was funded by people who wanted a reason to sue vaccine manufacturers and that he had withheld important information that would have changed the outcome of the study; for instance, he hid the fact that some of the children who took part in the study had developmental disorders before they ever received vaccines. The paper was discredited, and Wakefield was banned from practicing medicine.

A 2013 study by the CDC further proved this rumor false. The study followed children from birth until the age of three and documented their vaccinations. It showed that children with ASD and children without it received the same number of antigens (the part of a vaccine that makes the immune system create disease-fighting antibodies) from vaccines. All children had the same number of antigens, but some were diagnosed with autism and some were not. This proves that the antigens in vaccines do not cause autism.

Detecting Autism in Babies

Sally Ozonoff of the M.I.N.D. Institute is looking for other kinds of autism markers. She is trying to identify behaviors in the first year of life that can diagnose autism risk. She explained, "Behavioral science over the last 40 years has provided very reliable indicators of autism starting at age 2 or 3. We are determining the behavioral indicators to reliably diagnose autism earlier—maybe even as early as 12 months of age."[44] To find ways to detect autism in babies, researchers study the infant siblings of individuals already diagnosed with autism. If one child has autism, the younger siblings have a 20 percent chance of developing autism before their third birthday. In 2008, Ozonoff reported that 12-month-old babies could already show symptoms of autism. She studied 66 babies born to families who already had 1 child diagnosed with ASD. She chose these children because autism can run in families. She predicted that at least some of these babies would develop autism later in life. Ozonoff gave all the babies simple toys to play with and videotaped their responses. Nine of these babies did develop autism by the time they were three years old, and seven of them had played with their toys in a repetitive way. They spun and rotated the toys. They also did things such as look at the toys out of the corners of their eyes or stare intently at them for a long time. These behaviors almost never occurred in the babies who did not develop autism. Ozonoff said, "We wanted to directly test whether or not repetitive behaviors so characteristic of autism might actually be apparent earlier and therefore useful in early diagnosis ... Our results suggest that these particular behaviors might be useful to include in screening tests."[45]

Researchers hope to one day be able to diagnose autism in children as young as 12 months old.

Focusing on Ability

When it comes to the workforce, people with autism are often at a disadvantage. Many companies are unable to look past their disability. However, companies such as Aspiratech, a software-testing company in Illinois, focus on the abilities of their employees. Aspiratech hires adults with high-functioning (level one) autism as software testers. These adults get to use their strengths—extreme focus, repetition, and a detailed memory—to help other companies test out new computer programs or phone apps. Aspiratech provides its employees with a "relaxed environment" and hopes to be a starting point for adults with high functioning autism. Aspiritech's autism specialist Marc Lazar explained,

> We want to improve social skills among people who tend to be socially isolated. For many of them, software testing is not going to be their lifelong career, but while they're here they're going to improve their job skills and they're going to learn what kind of behavior is expected on the job and they're going to have more to put on their resumes.[1]

Several software-testing companies hire adults with high-functioning autism as software analysts or testers.

1. Quoted in Carla Johnson, "Startup Company Succeeds at Hiring Autistic Adults," *USA Today*, September 24, 2011. usatoday30.usatoday.com/money/smallbusiness/story/2011-09-24/autism-employment/50521438/1.

Many other studies look at certain infant behaviors or features that might indicate autism. One study showed that infants who have trouble with nonverbal communication such as pointing and making eye contact were more likely to be later diagnosed with autism. Another showed that poor motor control in infancy could indicate autism. Still another found that in infants as young as six months old, MRI technology can detect differences in white brain matter between those who would later go on to develop autism and those who would not. The study's co-author, Dr. Geraldine Dawson, said, "These results offer promise that we may one day be able to identify infants at risk for autism before the behavioral symptoms are present. The goal is to intervene as early as possible to prevent or reduce the onset of disabling symptoms."[46] Early diagnosis means that early intervention treatment could start even earlier. However, it still would not tell parents and clinicians which treatment is best.

The Medicinal Route

Some scientists' research suggests that the treatments of the future may be medicines and drug therapies. For example, Andrew Zimmerman of the Kennedy Krieger Institute in Baltimore, Maryland, studied the brains of people with autism after they had died. He and his team discovered that the brains were often irritated and inflamed and that they had high levels of certain proteins that do not occur in typical brains. In the future, drug therapies targeting specific areas of the brain might be able to change these conditions. In 2006, another Kennedy Krieger researcher, Elaine Tierney, found low levels of cholesterol in a small subgroup of children with autism. She said this finding suggests their bodies have a limited ability to make cholesterol. She believes that this might be a cause of autism for some because cholesterol is important to brain functioning.

At the University of California, Los Angeles, Alcino Silva and his research team tested the drug rapamycin on laboratory mice that had a kind of rare disease that also occurs in people. The disease is tuberous sclerosis complex and is caused by a malfunctioning gene. It causes severe intellectual disabilities, and more than half the people with this disease also have autism. The mice given rapamycin improved dramatically in their ability to learn and remember mazes. In 2008, Silva remarked, "This is the first study to demonstrate that the drug rapamycin can repair learning deficits related to a genetic mutation that causes autism in humans. The same mutation in animals produces learning disorders, which we were able to eliminate in adult mice."[47] In 2013, Boston Children's Hospital started a clinical trial to test rapamycin in children. As of 2017, some of the children in the study have reported improvements in language, memory, and attention span. If the trial's outcome is positive, rapamycin could become the first drug to treat ASD.

As of 2017, no medications have been developed that can cure ASD or treat its main symptoms. Some medicines may help with some of autism's associated medical problems or symptoms. For example, individuals with autism who experience depression or seizures can often benefit from medications to help reduce those symptoms. Individuals who experience violent tantrums or self-injury may benefit from a drug called risperidone. Risperidone is the first drug approved by the FDA to specifically treat a symptom of autism. However, *Scientific American* warned that the drug has "significant drawbacks and limitations. Not all people respond to it, symptoms often return when the drug is discontinued, and it doesn't improve many of the core behaviors associated with autism."[48] Additionally, it can have severe side effects, such as sleepiness and increased appetite leading to weight gain.

Support for Neurodiversity

Some people with high-functioning autism vigorously object to the treatment goals of researchers and groups such as Autism Speaks. There are no people with autism in the organization, so many adults living with autism feel as though they are not being represented by Autism Speaks. Many have different views and goals than the organization. Writer David Perry wrote in an article for the *New York Times*, "I have yet to meet an autistic person, either virtually or face-to-face, who supports Autism Speaks … my wife made the analogy that Autism Speaks was like an organization run entirely by boys, that got lots of money for saying that girls were bad and had to stop looking or acting like girls, and didn't have any girls involved."[49] Many people with autism oppose the idea of needing a cure for the disorder and would instead prefer for the focus to be on acceptance and understanding.

Amanda Baggs, a woman with autism, says she wants to change society, not herself. She does not want to "act more normal." She wants society to value her as a person. Just because, for example, she writes better than she speaks, she does not want her difficulties to be seen as "defects." She knows that she is different, but she does not want autism to be "eliminated," prevented, or cured. She explained,

I … know what it's like to not have a job or attend conventional school, to need a substantial amount of assistance in day-to-day life, to not be married, to not relate well to people, to have a decreased sense of danger, to not be able to talk, and so on. But these things, although they are quoted as being the source of pain to many parents, are much less of a source of pain to me, and most of my pain in this respect is much more based in society—its prejudices and its unwillingness to accommodate people like me—than in autism. Even many of my intrinsic difficulties as an autistic person could fade into the background given the proper societal setting. Any pain that is related in some way to autism, I would still take any day compared to the idea of not being autistic. I like what I am, in all of its flawless imperfection.[50]

The Autistic Self Advocacy Network (ASAN) is a nonprofit organization founded by people with autism to advocate for themselves. Its mission statement is, "Nothing About Us Without Us," indicating that people with autism who are part of the organization do not want decisions to be made for them without their input and approval. ASAN supports neurodiversity, and many people with autism say neurodiversity gives them a better self-image. John Elder Robison, an author and the Neurodiversity Scholar in Residence at the College of William & Mary in Williamsburg, Virginia, explained,

> *As an adult with autism, I find the idea of natural variation to be more appealing than the alternative—the suggestion that I am innately bad, or broken and in need of repair. I didn't learn about my own autism until I reached middle age. All those (pre diagnosis) years I assumed my struggles stemmed from inherent deficiencies. Asserting that I am different—not defective—is a much healthier position to take. Realizing the idea is supported by science is even better.*[51]

Philip Reyes feels the same: "I feel loved when I am accepted. I feel loved when I am seen not by my momentary deficits but by my attributes that make me a complete person. I think living with autism is no better or worse than living a typical life. Each life is special in its own way. I love my life with autism."[52]

The Future of Autism

A combination of genes, experiences, and relationships helps create someone's identity. For many individuals living with a chronic medical condition, that condition remains a central part of their identity. This is true for many of those living with autism. The future of autism may involve a cure, an environment where those with autism can have their needs met, or both.

On World Autism Day 2016, U.S. President Barack Obama spoke to the value each person with ASD brings to the world. He said,

> *From home to school and in businesses and communities around the world, people living with autism spectrum disorder contribute in immeasurable ways to our society. They remind us each day that every person is born with unique talents and should be treated with respect, play an active role in planning for their futures, and feel empowered to fully participate in and contribute to their communities. When those with autism have access to equal opportunities, we all do better, and that begins with making sure our country lives up to its commitment to ensure all things are possible for all people.*[53]

World landmarks, such as these pyramids in Egypt, light up blue in honor of World Autism Day each year.

Right now, the immediate future of autism is a world that focuses on the abilities, potential, and uniqueness of each child, adolescent, and adult with autism spectrum disorder. Children can look past differences in their classmates with autism and build friendships with them. People can stop staring when a child with autism has a public tantrum or flaps their arms. Employers can focus on creating inclusive hiring practices that do not discriminate against those with social challenges. Research must continue because there are still so many unanswered questions, whose answers will help the millions of individuals living with ASD.

Obama ended his speech with a statement that speaks to this idea of the future of autism: "Today, and every day, let us reach for a future in which no person living on the autism spectrum is limited by anything but the size of their dreams—one in which all people have the opportunity to live a life filled with a sense of identity, purpose, and self-determination."[54]

NOTES

Introduction: The Autism Puzzle

1. Quoted in Ruth Padawer, "The Kids Who Beat Autism," *New York Times*, July 31, 2014. www.nytimes.com/2014/08/03/magazine/the-kids-who-beat-autism.html.

Chapter One: A Glimpse at Autism

2. Ron Suskind, "Reaching My Autistic Son Through Disney," *New York Times*, March 7, 2014. www.nytimes.com/2014/03/09/magazine/reaching-my-autistic-son-through-disney.html.

3. Temple Grandin, *Thinking in Pictures and Other Reports from My Life with Autism*. New York, NY: Doubleday, 1995, p. 43.

4. Donna Williams, *Nobody Nowhere: The Extraordinary Autobiography of an Autistic*. New York, NY: Avon, 1992, pp. 3–4.

5. "Autism Spectrum Disorder," National Institute of Mental Health, October 2016. www.nimh.nih.gov/health/topics/autism-spectrum-disorders-asd/index.shtml.

6. Karen Wang, "What You Need to Know About Echolalia," Friendship Circle—Special Needs Resources, April 18, 2012. www.friendshipcircle.org/blog/2012/04/18/what-you-need-to-know-about-echolalia/.

7. Quoted in Paul Karasik and Judy Karasik, *The Ride Together: A Brother and Sister's Memoir of Autism in the Family*. New York, NY: Washington Square, 2003, p. 115.

8. Quoted in Lisa Reyes, "I Have Nonverbal Autism. Here's What I Want You to Know," *The Mighty*, April 6, 2015. themighty.com/2015/04/i-have-nonverbal-autism-heres-what-i-want-you-to-know/.

9. "Fragile X Syndrome," U.S. National Library of Medicine, April 4, 2017. ghr.nlm.nih.gov/condition/fragile-x-syndrome.

10. Quoted in Maureen Salamon, "Adults with Autism at Risk for Many Health Problems," WebMD, May 14, 2014. www.webmd.com/brain/autism/news/20140514/adults-with-autism-at-risk-for-many-health-problems-study#1.

Chapter Two: Diagnosing Autism

11. Quoted in Amy Lutz, "You Do Not Have Asperger's," *Slate*, May 22, 2013. www.slate.com/articles/health_and_science/medical_examiner/2013/05/autism_spectrum_diagnoses_the_dsm_5_eliminates_asperger_s_and_pdd_nos.html.

12. Quoted in *"DSM-5* Diagnostic Criteria," Autism Speaks, 2013. www.autismspeaks.org/what-autism/diagnosis/dsm-5-diagnostic-criteria.

13. Quoted in "Autism Spectrum Disorder Diagnostic Criteria," Centers for Disease Control and Prevention, 2013. www.cdc.gov/ncbddd/autism/hcp-dsm.html.

14. Jamie M. Kleinman et al., "The Modified Checklist for Autism in Toddlers: A Followup Study Investigating the Early Detection of Autism Spectrum Disorders," *Journal of Autism and Developmental Disorders*, vol. 38, 2008, pp. 827–839.

15. "Autism Information Center: Screening and Diagnosis," Centers for Disease Control and Prevention, February 7, 2007. www.cdc.gov/ncbddd/autism/screening.html.

16. Lutz, "You Do Not have Asperger's."

Chapter Three: Causes of Autism

17. Quoted in "Unlocking Autism's Mysteries," Carnegie Mellon University, March 6, 2012. www.cmu.edu/news/stories/archives/2012/march/march6_brainautism.html.

18. "Born Different: What Causes Asperger's Syndrome?," *Asperger's Syndrome*, Encyclopedia.com, 2009. www.encyclopedia.com/science/medical-magazines/born-different-what-causes-aspergers-syndrome.

19. Uta Frith and Elisabeth Hill, *Autism: Mind and Brain*. New York, NY: Oxford University Press, 2004, p. 5.

20. Quoted in "Ground-Breaking Studies Discover Brain Differences in Autism," AutismConnect News, December 7, 2006. www.autismconnect.org/news.asp?-section=00010001 &itemtype=news&id=5816.

21. Grandin, *Thinking in Pictures*, p. 19.

22. Quoted in "Autism's Social Struggles Due to Disrupted Communication Networks in Brain," e! Science News, July 23, 2008. esciencenews.com/articles/2008/07/23/autisms.social.struggles.due.disrupted.communication.networks.brain.

23. Quoted in Daniel J. DeNoon, "Autism Cause: Brain Development Genes?," WebMD, July 10, 2008. www.webmd.com/brain/autism/news/20080710/autism-cause-brain-development-genes.

24. "Spontaneous Gene Glitches Linked to Autism Risk with Older Dads," National Institute of Mental Health, April 4, 2012. www.nimh.nih.gov/news/science-news/2012/spontaneous-gene-glitches-linked-to-autism-risk-with-older-dads.shtml.

25. Simon Baron-Cohen, "Linking Autism, Sex, Gender and Prenatal Hormones," *Spectrum*, October 19, 2015. spectrumnews.org/opinion/linking-autism-sex-gender-and-prenatal-hormones/.

26. Quoted in Nidhi Subbaraman, "Study on 'Extreme Male Brain' Theory of Autism Draws Critics," *Spectrum*, August 25, 2014. spectrumnews.org/news/study-on-extreme-male-brain-theory-of-autism-draws-critics/.

27. Janelle Weaver, "Why Autism Strikes More Boys than Girls," *Scientific American*, July 1, 2011. www.scientificamerican.com/article/why-autism-strikes-more-boys-than-girls/.

Chapter Four: Treatment Options

28. Quoted in Jane Weaver, "Inside the Autism Treatment Maze," MSNBC.com, August 9, 2005. www.msnbc.msn.com/id/6948119.

29. "Autism FAQ," Autism Society of America. www.autism-society.org/site/PageServer?pagename=about_FAQ.

30. Quoted in Teresa J. Foden and Connie Anderson, "Social Skills Interventions: Getting to the Core of Autism," Interactive Autism Network, January 16, 2009. www.iancommunity.org/cs/what_do_we_know/social_skills_interventions.

31. Quoted in Elizabeth Picciuto, "They Don't Want an Autism Cure," The Daily Beast. www.thedailybeast.com/articles/2015/02/25/they-don-t-want-an-autism-cure.html.

32. Quoted in Reyes, "I Have Nonverbal Autism."

33. "DIR and the DIRFloortime Approach," Interdisciplinary Council on Developmental and Learning Disorders. www.icdl.com/DIR.

34. "Capacity 3: Purposeful Two-Way Communication," Interdisciplinary Council on Developmental and Learning Disorders. www.icdl.com/DIR/6-developmental-milestones/stage-3-two-way-communication.

Chapter Five: Life with Autism

35. Grandin, Thinking in Pictures, p. 62.

36. Temple Grandin and Catherine Johnson, Animals in Translation: Using the Mysteries of Autism to Decode Animal Behavior. San Diego, CA: Houghton Mifflin Harcourt, 2006, pp. 4–5.

37. Grandin, Thinking in Pictures, p. 63.

38. Grandin, Thinking in Pictures, p. 63.

39. Grandin, Thinking in Pictures, pp. 60–61.

40. Kristin Stanberry, "Understanding Individualized Education Programs," Understood. www.understood.org/en/school-learning/special-services/ieps/understanding-individualized-education-programs.

Chapter Six: The Road to a Cure

41. "Mission," Autism Speaks. www.autismspeaks.org/about-us/mission.

42. Annetta Miller, "Gene Mapping is Now Unlocking the Mysteries of Autism," CNBC, April 26, 2016. www.cnbc.com/2016/04/26/gene-mapping-is-now-unlocking-the-mysteries-of-autism.html.

43. David G. Amaral, "Welcome to the Autism Phenome Project!" UC Davis M.I.N.D. Institute. www.ucdmc.ucdavis.edu/mindinstitute/research/app/amaralwelcome.html.

44. Quoted in Karen Finney, "Autism Experts to Be Featured on CBS," UC Newsroom, February 15, 2007. www.university ofcalifornia.edu/news/article/8923.

45. Quoted in "Unusual Use of Toys in Infancy a Clue to Later Autism," UC Davis Health, November 6, 2008. www.ucdmc.ucdavis.edu/publish/news/newsroom/1344.

46. Quoted in "Researchers See Differences in Autism Brain Development as Early as 6 Months," Autism Speaks, February 17, 2012. www.autismspeaks.org/science/science-news/researchers-see-differences-autism-brain-development-early-6-months.

47. "Drug Reverses Mental Retardation Caused by Genetic Disorder; Hope for Correcting How Autism Disrupts Brain," *ScienceDaily*, University of California–Los Angeles, June 23, 2008. www.sciencedaily.com/releases/2008/06/080622224428.htm.

48. Emily Anthes, "Widely Used Autism Drug Carries Heavy Risks for Children," *Scientific American*, May 8, 2014. www.scientificamerican.com/article/widely-used-autism-drug-carries-heavy-risks-for-children/.

49. David Perry, "Speaking Out Against Autism Speaks, Even if It Means No Ice Cream," *New York Times*, June 4, 2015. parenting.blogs.nytimes.com/2015/06/04/speaking-out-against-autism-speaks-even-if-it-means-no-ice-cream/.

50. Amanda Baggs, "Love, Devotion, Hope, Prevention, and Cure," Autism Information Library, Autistics.org. www.autistics.org/library/love.html.

51. John Elder Robison, "What Is Neurodiversity?," *Psychology Today*, October 7, 2013. www.psychologytoday.com/blog/my-life-aspergers/201310/what-is-neurodiversity.

52. Quoted in Reyes, "I Have Nonverbal Autism."

53. Barack Obama, "Presidential Proclamation: World Autism Awareness Day, 2016," WhiteHouse.gov, April 2, 2016. www.whitehouse.gov/the-press-office/2016/04/01/presidential-proclamation-world-autism-awareness-day-2016.

54. Barack Obama, "Presidential Proclamation: World Autism Awareness Day, 2016."

amygdala: The part of brain involved in how humans feel emotions.

applied behavior analysis (ABA): A scientifically designed treatment method that uses a system of rewards to teach specific behaviors and skills and to reduce unwanted behaviors.

brain plasticity: The ability of the brain to rewire and change its organization because of learning experiences, especially in the first few years of life.

child development: The complex process of change that all human beings go through beginning at birth as they learn to move, think, feel, and relate to other people.

corpus callosum: The nerve tissue that connects the two hemispheres of the brain and allows them to communicate with each other.

deoxyribonucleic acid (DNA): The chemicals in the genes that carry the coding instructions for all the body's structures and functions.

DIRFloortime: A treatment method that emphasizes emotional relationships and engaging a child's interests at his or her level of ability while socially interacting intensely with the child.

echolalia: The repetition or parroting of words or phrases spoken by others.

gene: A discrete segment of DNA on a specific point of a chromosome that carries a specific unit of inheritance.

genome: The complete genetic material of an organism, which includes its DNA and RNA.

nonverbal: Having no communication in words; without spoken language.

phenotypic trait: The observable expression of an organism's genes, such as eye color, skin color, or behavior.

prognosis: The predicted outcome of something.

self-stimulation: Repetitive body movements or behaviors, generally known as "stimming."

Association for Science in Autism Treatment (ASAT)
PO Box 1447
Hoboken, NJ 07030
info@asatonline.org
www.asatonline.org
ASAT is dedicated to improving the education, care, and treatment of people with autism. It is especially concerned with identifying questionable treatments and cures and helping families get scientifically supported, accurate information.

Autism Spectrum Disorder (ASD):
Centers for Disease Control and Prevention (CDC)
1600 Clifton Rd.
Atlanta, GA 30329
(800) 232-4636
www.cdc.gov/ncbddd/autism/index.html
At this government website, visitors can find information about ASD, downloadable fact sheets, and general publications. The CDC conducts and funds research into all aspects of ASD.

Autism Society of America (ASA)
4340 East-West Hwy
Suite 350
Bethesda, MD 20814
(800) 328-8476
www.autism-society.org
ASA is a national organization founded by doctors Bernard Rimland and Ruth Sullivan. The society dedicates itself to improving the lives of people with autism, providing information to parents and families, and politically advocating for those with autism.

Organization for Autism Research (OAR)
2000 N 14th St.
Suite 240
Arlington, VA 22201
(866) 366-9710
www.researchautism.org
OAR focuses on funding research that examines the challenges individuals living with ASD face daily and sharing the results of that research in ways that will help make their lives easier.

Books

Bleach, Fiona. *Everybody Is Different: A Book for Young People Who Have Brothers or Sisters with Autism.* London, UK: The National Autistic Society, 2001.
This nontechnical, simply written book answers many questions that young people may have about a sibling with autism.

Durà-Vilà, Glòria, and Tamar Levi. *My Autism Book: A Child's Guide to Their Autism Spectrum Diagnosis.* Philadelphia, PA: Jessica Kingsley Publishers, 2014.
This book helps parents explain to their children with autism what an ASD diagnosis means.

Grandin, Temple. *Thinking in Pictures, Expanded Edition: My Life with Autism.* New York, NY: Vintage Books, 2006.
In her book, Grandin reveals how she experiences the world as both a person with autism and a scientist.

Shaul, Joel. *Our Brains Are Like Computers!: Exploring Social Skills and Social Cause and Effect with Children on the Autism Spectrum.* Philadelphia, PA: Jessica Kingsley Publishers, 2016.
People with autism have a difficult time with social interaction. This book discusses social skills in a way that many people with autism can relate to.

Suskind, Ron. *Life, Animated: A Story of Sidekicks, Heroes, and Autism.* Glendale, CA: Kingswell, 2014.
This *New York Times* bestseller tells the story of Owen Suskind, the author's son with autism, and how he used dialogue and characters from Disney movies to communicate with his family.

Websites

Donna Williams
www.donnawilliams.net
Williams discusses her autism and the effect it has had
on her life, shares her art and poetry, and maintains a
personal blog.

Interagency Autism Coordinating Committee (IACC)
iacc.hhs.gov
The IACC website provides updates on the latest
autism research advancements and on the work the
IACC is doing with the Department of Health and
Human Services.

Neuroscience for Kids
faculty.washington.edu/chud ler/introb.html.
At this website from the University of Washington,
visitors can learn all about the brain, its lobes, and
its wiring.

Spectrum News
spectrumnews.org
Spectrum News provides readers with news and opinions
on the latest advances in autism research.

Temple Grandin, Ph.D.
www.templegrandin.com
Visitors to Dr. Grandin's website can learn about her
experience living with autism, the books she has written
about autism, and the many conferences she speaks at
each year.

Wrong Planet
www.wrongplanet.net
Wrong Planet provides those living with ASD a place to
post in online forums and read member-written articles
about autism and different aspects of life. Always ask a
parent or guardian before taking part in a forum.

Sarah Goldy-Brown holds a Bachelor of Arts degree in public relations from Messiah College. She currently lives in a small town outside of Allentown, Pennsylvania, where she enjoys freelance writing. Sarah became interested in neurological conditions after being diagnosed with post-concussion syndrome. This is her first publication.